Blender Quick Start

3D Modeling, Animation, and Render with Eevee
in Blender 2.8

Allan Brito

BIRMINGHAM - MUMBAI

Blender Quick Start Guide

Commissioning Editor: Kunal Chaudhari
Acquisition Editor: Reshma Raman
Content Development Editor: Roshan Kumar
Technical Editor: Jinesh Topiwala
Copy Editor: Safis Editing
Project Coordinator: Hardik Bhinde
Proofreader: Safis Editing
Indexer: Pratik Shirodkar
Graphics: Alishon Mendonsa
Production Coordinator: Shantanu Zagade

First published: September 2018

Production reference: 1280918

Published by Packt Publishing Ltd.
Livery Place
35 Livery Street
Birmingham
B3 2PB, UK.

ISBN 978-1-78961-947-8

www.packtpub.com

To my newborn son Arthur, for giving me a reason to become a better person every day for the rest of my life.

-Allan Brito

`mapt.io`

Mapt is an online digital library that gives you full access to over 5,000 books and videos, as well as industry leading tools to help you plan your personal development and advance your career. For more information, please visit our website.

Why subscribe?

- Spend less time learning and more time coding with practical eBooks and videos from over 4,000 industry professionals

- Improve your learning with Skill Plans built especially for you

- Get a free eBook or video every month

- Mapt is fully searchable

- Copy and paste, print, and bookmark content

Packt.com

Did you know that Packt offers eBook versions of every book published, with PDF and ePub files available? You can upgrade to the eBook version at `www.packt.com` and as a print book customer, you are entitled to a discount on the eBook copy. Get in touch with us at `customercare@packtpub.com` for more details.

At `www.packt.com`, you can also read a collection of free technical articles, sign up for a range of free newsletters, and receive exclusive discounts and offers on Packt books and eBooks.

Contributors

About the author

Allan Brito is an architect with a strong background in the use of technology in all phases of project development. His friends used to say that he swapped bricks for pixels.

Besides working in the architecture business, he also has more than 10 years, experience as a college teacher, helping students to create animations, 3D games, and mobile apps.

In the academic field, he was in charge of the e-learning department of one of the largest colleges in Brazil for almost eight years, using technologies such as interactive 3D content, games, and virtual reality as learning tools.

Blender is one of the essential tools in his workflow, and he has used it every day since 2005 with version 2.35.

About the reviewers

Fernando Castilhos Melo lives in Toronto, Canada, and works as a software engineer. Since 2009, he has used his spare time to work on 3D modeling using Blender. He has lectured on Blender and 3D modeling at several Brazilian free/open source software events.

Fernando holds a degree in computer science from UCS (Universidade de Caxias do Sul, Brazil), and this is the fourth Blender book that he has worked on. The other ones were *Blender Cycles: Lighting and Rendering Cookbook,* in 2013; *Blender 3D by Example,* in 2015; and *Blender 3D Printing by Example,* in 2017.

Moreover, he has also developed an integration between Blender and Kinect named *Kinected Blender* to generate 3D animations using body movements captured from Kinect.

> *I would like to send a big **thank you** to the following people:*
> *– My wife, Mauren, for all the support she gave me during this reviewing process*
> *– My parents, Eloir and Miriam, for encouraging me*
> *– My dog, Polly, for being (literally) at my side all the time during this review*
> *– All my friends for giving me the confidence to carry out this work*

Germano Cavalcante de Sousa, with a background in architecture, uses Blender for arch viz work.

He has developed add-ons aimed at architecture, including the `snap_utilities_line` add-on, which is officially distributed with Blender. He also helps, when he can, in Blender development, focusing on transformation and snapping capabilities.

> *I would like to thank Allan Brito for referring me for the book review and Hardik Bhinde for coordinating the review work.*

Packt is searching for authors like you

If you're interested in becoming an author for Packt, please visit `authors.packtpub.com` and apply today. We have worked with thousands of developers and tech professionals, just like you, to help them share their insights with the global tech community. You can make a general application, apply for a specific hot topic that we are recruiting an author for, or submit your own idea.

Table of Contents

Preface

Blender has a long history in the computer graphics industry, but has not always been associated with quality content or ease of use. If you do a quick survey about the software among artists, you would get mixed opinions, with some criticism being aimed at the user interface. People would say it is hard to use or is missing powerful features.

In the last five years, the software has received significant updates on various tools, especially in the user interface. Blender has now been reborn with a brand new batch of software, features that match some multi-million-dollar tools on the market, and an interface that has improved usability.

And all that at no cost! In the era of subscription-based software, Blender is still free and open source. You can download the software at no cost and use it on as many computers as you want.

In this book, you will find a quick introduction to most of the new features of Blender 2.8, such as the fantastic real-time render engine Eevee and the revamped user interface.

Who this book is for

Digital artists or hobbyists who are looking to use Blender as a tool to create realistic 3D graphics for animation, video, games, or printed media would benefit from this book. The objective of this book is to give a quick explanation of the core concepts and mechanics of Blender.

With a sound knowledge of these topics, you will quickly be able to produce 3D content with Blender.

What this book covers

Chapter 1, *Using Blender 2.8 UI, Shading and Navigator Widget*, will start with the brand new user interface of Blender and some of the most acclaimed features, such as the new shading system. You will also find instructions on how to manipulate windows and do some 3D navigation.

Chapter 2, *3D Modeling and Real-Time Rendering in Eevee*, gives you the tools needed to create 3D models based on polygons. After creating some models, we will dive into rendering with the new options present in Blender 2.8.

Chapter 3, *The New 3D Cursor and Modeling Options*, shows how you can use a unique tool from Blender called 3D Cursor. At first, you might find it strange, but after a few minutes, you will find it an impressive productivity tool for 3D modeling. Besides the cursor, you will also learn about additional tools, such as modifiers.

Chapter 4, *Using Real-Time Materials in Eevee*, adds a layer of realism to your work by creating materials for your scenes. After learning how to craft materials, you will get to develop surfaces such as glass and plastic.

Chapter 5, *Real-Time Textures for Eevee*, will raise the quality of your materials one step further. Better yet, a full staircase further! You will learn how to assign image-based textures to materials to craft what's known as PBR materials.

Chapter 6, *Lights and Real-Time Rendering with Blender Eevee*, gives you a better explanation of how to make use of the options for Eevee. The real-time engine in Blender 2.8 will provide you with better results through the use of environment textures and some post-processing effects.

Chapter 7, *Animate Everything in Blender 2.8!*, brings you all the tools that are necessary for creating animations with Blender. After you learn how to use interpolation-based animations in Blender, you will find it rather easy to start new projects and make small videos.

Chapter 8, *Editing Animations in Blender 2.8*, shows you some of the options for editing and changing the behavior of animations in Blender, such as setting a specific timing for a motion and creating animation loops.

To get the most out of this book

Before getting started, the following are stipulated as requirements:

- Download Blender from the Blender Foundation website: https://www.blender.org
- Get yourself a computer with a mouse
- That's it! You don't need any prior experience with Blender! We will start from scratch

Download the example code files

You can download the example code files for this book from your account at www.packtpub.com. If you purchased this book elsewhere, you can visit www.packtpub.com/support and register to have the files emailed directly to you.

You can download the code files by following these steps:

1. Log in or register at www.packtpub.com.
2. Select the **SUPPORT** tab.
3. Click on **Code Downloads & Errata**.
4. Enter the name of the book in the **Search** box and follow the onscreen instructions.

Once the file is downloaded, please make sure that you unzip or extract the folder using the latest version of:

- WinRAR/7-Zip for Windows
- Zipeg/iZip/UnRarX for Mac
- 7-Zip/PeaZip for Linux

The code bundle for the book is also hosted on GitHub at https://github.com/PacktPublishing/Blender-Quick-Start-Guide. In case there's an update to the code, it will be updated on the existing GitHub repository.

We also have other code bundles from our rich catalog of books and videos available at https://github.com/PacktPublishing/. Check them out!

Download the color images

We also provide a PDF file that has color images of the screenshots/diagrams used in this book. You can download it here:
http://www.packtpub.com/sites/default/files/downloads/9781789619478_ColorImages.pdf.

Code in action

Visit the following link to check out videos of the code being run:

bit.ly/2R4ghUh.

Conventions used

There are a number of text conventions used throughout this book.

`CodeInText`: Indicates code words in text, database table names, folder names, filenames, file extensions, pathnames, dummy URLs, user input, and Twitter handles. Here is an example: "On your keyboard, type `0.2` as a value and press *Enter*."

Bold: Indicates a new term, an important word, or words that you see on screen. For example, words in menus or dialog boxes appear in the text like this. Here is an example: "Once you change to **Edit Mode**, you will see a few different options in the 3D view."

Warnings or important notes appear like this.

Tips and tricks appear like this.

Get in touch

Feedback from our readers is always welcome.

General feedback: If you have questions about any aspect of this book, mention the book title in the subject of your message and email us at `customercare@packt.com`.

Errata: Although we have taken every care to ensure the accuracy of our content, mistakes do happen. If you have found a mistake in this book, we would be grateful if you would report this to us. Please visit `www.packt.com/submit-errata`, selecting your book, clicking on the Errata Submission Form link, and entering the details.

Piracy: If you come across any illegal copies of our works in any form on the internet, we would be grateful if you would provide us with the location address or website name. Please contact us at `copyright@packt.com` with a link to the material.

If you are interested in becoming an author: If there is a topic that you have expertise in and you are interested in either writing or contributing to a book, please visit authors.packt.com.

Reviews

Please leave a review. Once you have read and used this book, why not leave a review on the site that you purchased it from? Potential readers can then see and use your unbiased opinion to make purchase decisions, we at Packt can understand what you think about our products, and our authors can see your feedback on their book. Thank you!

For more information about Packt, please visit packt.com.

1
Using Blender 2.8 UI, Shading and Navigator Widget

Finding your way around Blender is the first step to starting to create astonishing 3D models or animations with the software; knowing the interface is critical. In the following chapters, you will learn how to use and manipulate the new user interface of Blender 2.8, and some render options with the OpenGL options.

Blender 2.8 is a huge milestone for the software and you will get to know a lot of the new tools, like the new Eevee renderer. You will also learn how to create 3D models using polygons and even create a quick animation using 3D text.

This first chapter will focus on getting you around the interface! Here is a list of what you will learn:

- Managing the user interface
- 3D navigation
- Selecting objects
- Applying 3D transformations
- Using keyboard shortcuts in Blender

Technical requirements

You will be required to have Blender 2.80 installed to follow this procedure. Even if you have a later version of Blender, the described example should work with no significant problems.

The code files of this chapter can be found on GitHub:
`https://github.com/PacktPublishing/Blender-Quick-Start-Guide.`

Check out the following video to see the code in action:

`bit.ly/2IocoFW.`

The Blender user interface

When you open Blender for the first time, you will see what we call the default user interface. The interface in Blender is flexible to the point where you can stretch and reshape it in any way you want. The following screenshot shows the default user interface for Blender:

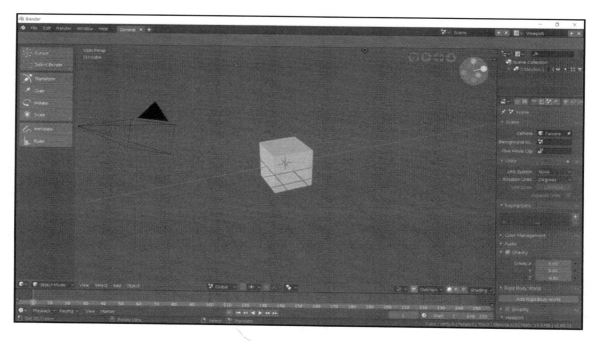

Figure 1.1: Default user interface

One of the core concepts about the interface is that it works with a window system. Each division of the interface is a window that you can resize and change based on context.

Resizing windows

To resize a window you have to place the mouse cursor between a division; once the cursor turns into a double arrow, you can left click and drag to resize the window, as shown in the following screenshot:

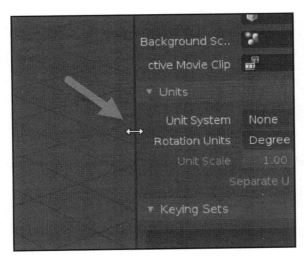

Figure 1.2: Resizing windows

Managing windows

The process of creating new windows in Blender is quite simple once you learn how to use the corners of the existing windows. Each of the four corners of a window will work as a reference for either splitting or merging windows.

If you move the mouse cursor to a corner, like the top right, you will see the cursor turning into a cross as shown in the next screenshot:

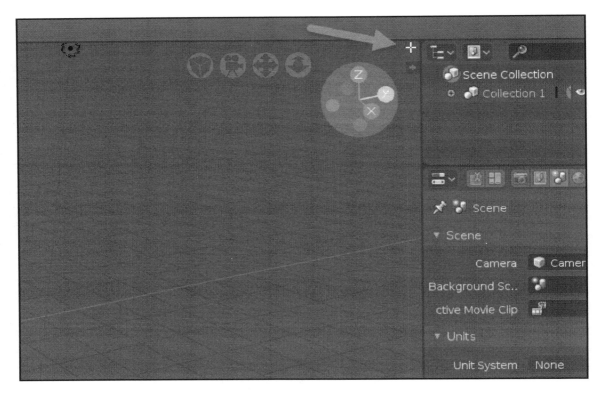

Figure 1.3: Cross at the corner

Once you have the cursor as a cross, you can left-click and drag the mouse towards the center of your actual window to create a division, shown as follows:

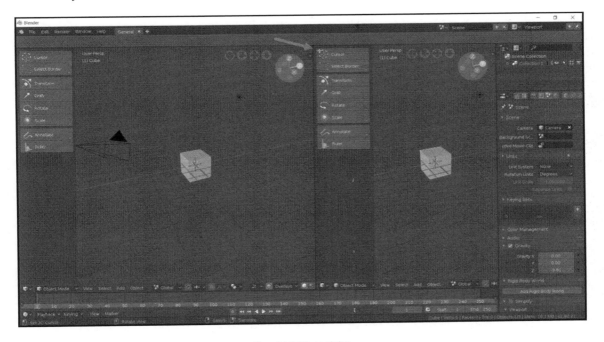

Figure 1.4: Splitting a window

You have two options to split windows:

- **Moving up or down**: Creates a horizontal division
- **Moving left or right**: Creates a vertical division

Merging windows

How do we merge windows? The process to join the two windows is the same we use to create a division. But, instead of dragging the cursor towards the center, you will move it to the window you want to merge.

There is a simple rule you have to follow to merge two windows successfully—both of them must share the same edge. The shared side must have the same size.

Here is an example of two windows that share the same edge:

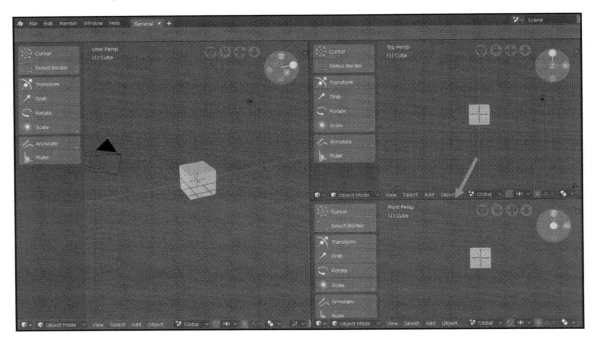

Figure 1.5: Windows with the same edge

If you place the mouse cursor in one of the corners for the shared edge, you will be able to left click and drag the cursor over the window that you want to disappear. Blender will help you by showing a big arrow pointing to the direction of the expanding window, shown in the next screenshot:

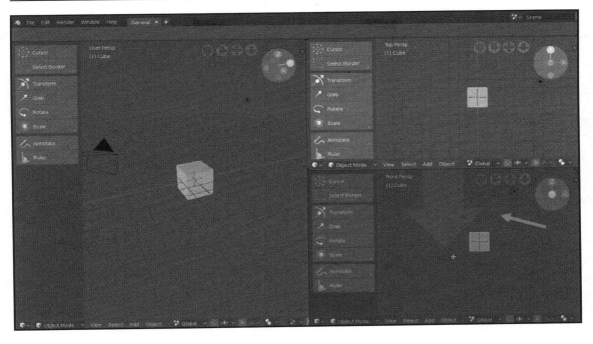

Figure 1.6: Merging windows

Active window and shortcuts

At this point, you already know how to manipulate windows, and we can move to the next core concept of Blender, which is the active window. Why is that important? Because it has a close relationship with another aspect of Blender, which is keyboard shortcuts.

Blender has a lot of keyboard shortcuts that will save you a tremendous amount of time for simple tasks. The relationship between windows and shortcuts is that you can choose where to call a tool using a shortcut on each window.

You can always work with a single window in Blender by maximizing the active window. Press the *Ctrl + Spacebar* keys to maximize any window.

For instance, you can create multiple divisions at the interface and have five views of an object in different 3D views, shown in the next screenshot. If you press the *G* Key to move an object, where you will control the translation?

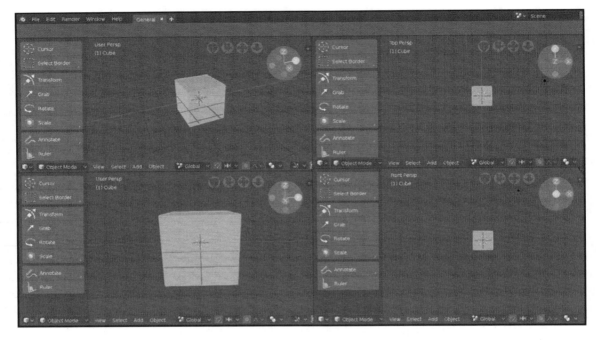

Figure 1.7: Multiple divisions

You will always control and use the tool in the active window. But what is the active window? That is the window where your mouse cursor is at the moment you call the hotkey.

That concept is important to know, because you may accidentally press a key when the wrong window is active.

With time and practice, you will unconsciously move the cursor to a window before hitting a key to perform a task in Blender.

Selecting objects

The next step to learn about Blender is how to select objects and transform them in 3D. To select an object, you can right click on them in the 3D View window. That is the window we use to see all objects in 3D, manipulate them, and do most of the visual work. You will see an orange border surrounding the selected objects, as shown in the following screenshot:

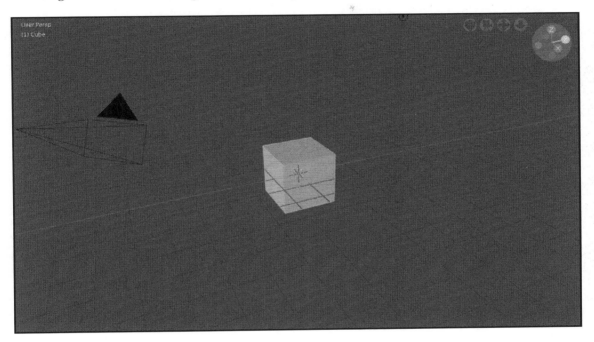

Figure 1.8: Selection in the 3D View

To deselect an object, you can hold the *Shift* key and right-click on any object, or use a shortcut. The shortcut to deselect any object is *Alt + A*.

 You must set the 3D View as your active window to use those shortcuts.

If you hold the *Shift* key and right-click on other objects, Blender will add them to the selection. You can click on as many objects as you need; note the following screenshot:

Figure 1.9: Multiple objects selected

Do you want to select all the objects in your scene? Just press the *A* key in the 3D View, and you will select all objects.

The color surrounding your selected objects may be different. Those colors come from the theme you use for the Blender user interface.

Another way to select multiple objects in Blender is with the **Select Border** tool. You can activate that tool using the *B* key or the icon in the toolbar at the left side of your 3D View.

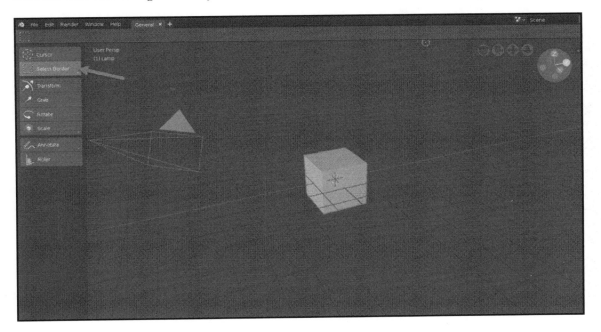

Figure 1.10: Select border

Using that tool you can draw a window around all objects that you want to select, as demonstrated in the next screenshot:

Figure 1.11: Border around objects

Transforming objects

In any 3D software like Blender, transformations play a significant role in the everyday tasks an artist will perform in the software. You will use them for anything, starting with 3D modeling and going all the way to animations.

The three fundamental transformations available are:

- Grab
- Rotate
- Scale

Blender will allow us to use several different ways to apply those transformations. The easiest way to implement them is with the transform gizmo. You can activate the gizmo using the options in the toolbar, as shown in the next screenshot:

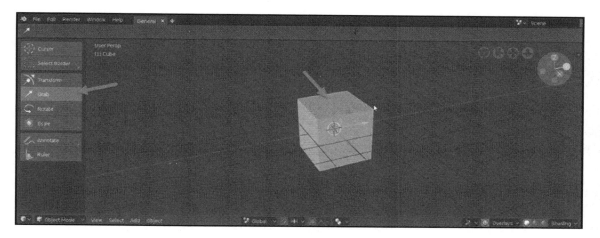

Figure 1.12: Transform gizmo

You can toggle the toolbar in the 3D View using the *T* key. If you can't see it in your interface, press the *T* key, and it will appear.

Moving objects

Let's start with the second option, which is the **Grab** tool. If you select an object (right-click) and press the **Grab** button, you will see the transform gizmo with multiple arrows.

Each arrow has a color code that shows:

- Red arrow: Move in the *x* axis
- Green arrow: Move in the *y* axis
- Blue arrow: Move in the *z* axis

For transformations, the color codes won't change, and you will always find red, green, and blue as *x*, *y*, and *z* respectively.

Now, you can left-click at any arrow and keep the button pressed, dragging the mouse. You will be able to translate the object around. Blender will constrain the movement to the axis of the arrow you have clicked, as illustrated in the next screenshot:

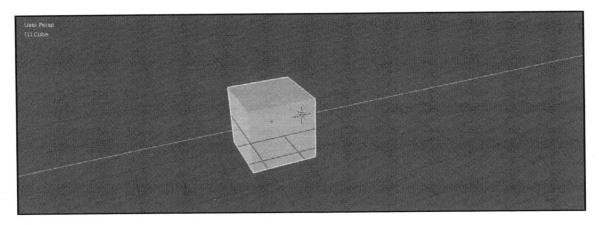

Figure 1.13: Object moving

Is there a faster way to move objects? You can also use the *G* key when you have an object selected. It will trigger the move tool.

But, you will notice something different about the *G* key. It will not constrain the translation of our object to any axis. You will be able to move it around freely.

We can also constrain the move operation to an axis by pressing the key equivalent to that axis, right after you press the *G* key.

For instance, if you press the *G* key and right after press the *X* key, you will constraint the move to the *x* axis.

Blender will even give you a list of suggestions for possible tools and options in the status bar at the bottom of your interface. There you will see a list of all possible shortcuts for a given tool, as indicated in the next screenshot:

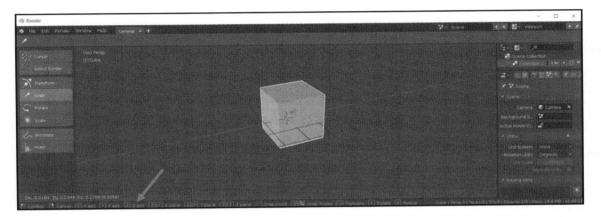

Figure 1.14: Options for moving objects

Always look at the status bar to find relative hotkeys for a tool you are using with Blender, in case you can't remember the key.

Rotating objects

Using the same principle from what you already know about transformations, we can rotate objects by either utilizing the toolbar button or with a hotkey. If you press the *R* key, you will start to rotate objects.

However, you will find that the gizmo for rotations is different from the one used to move objects. Replacing the arrows, you will get arcs with the same color code for each axis, as shown in the next screenshot:

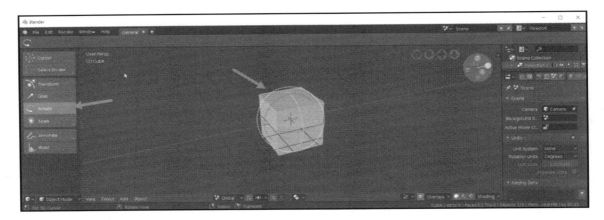

Figure 1.15: Rotate gizmo

By using the right mouse button to click and drag each arc, you will rotate an object. That will constrain the transformation to a single axis.

With the *R* key, you will get rotation for the object that doesn't have any axis reference. As with the move tool, you can use the status bar to find additional options for the rotation. Press the *R* key and right after that press the *X*, *Y*, or *Z* keys to constraint the rotation to a single axis, shown as follows:

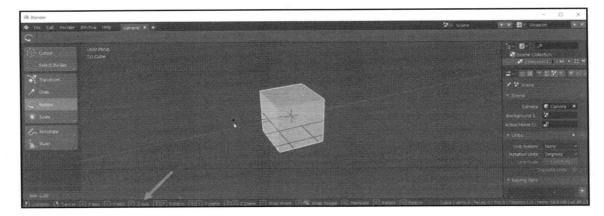

Figure 1.16: Rotation options

1.5.3 Scaling objects

For the scaling objects, you get the same options; you can either use the button on the toolbar or use the *S*-key shortcut. Using the button on the toolbar will give you immediate options to constrain the scale to a single axis.

To get the same results with the *S* key, you can use the *X*, *Y*, or *Z* keys.

What about the first button? If you click at the **Transform** button in the toolbar you will get a widget that has all .

Shading options for Blender 2.8

With a solid base to select and transform objects in Blender, we can move further and get around shading. Until now you probably just used the basic shading options from the default user interface.

In Blender 2.8 you will get a lot of options for shading at the bottom of the 3D View (Figure 1.17), shown as follows:

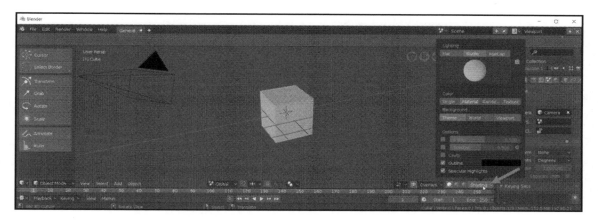

Figure 1.17: Shading options

To fully see everything we can do with shading options in Blender, you have to create more than merely a cube. So let us try duplicating the cube and apply the shading options:

1. To duplicate the cube, select the cube that is present and press *Shift + D* key
2. Now that the cube has been duplicated, we will align the copy above the original by pressing the Z key and placing the new cube right above the first cube. Blender will move the new object right after you press the keys, and you can constrain the copy on any axis.
3. Repeat the process till you get three cubes aligned in the Z axis shown in the below screenshot.

Use your mouse wheel or the - and + keys from your numeric keyboard to zoom in and out of your 3D View.

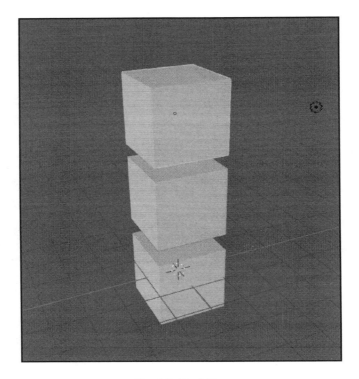

Figure 1.18: Aligned objects

You can always cancel any transformation using the *Esc* key. If you press the *Esc* key during a duplication, it will place the new copy at the same position as the original object. To erase the copy, you can do an Undo with the *Ctrl* + *Z* keys.

They all appear with a flat color in your 3D View, and we can change that using some shading options, which will be important later when we start to use Eevee to render in real time.

There are three primary locations to adjust your shading in Blender: **Lighting, Color**, and **Options**.

In the lighting field you will see three buttons:

- **Flat**: The most straightforward option that will display a flat light with no volumetric options.
- **Studio**: Here we have a simulation of a studio setup with an infinite background and area lights to the sides.
- **MatCap**: This is short for *Material Capture* and will display a realistic shading for a surface based on reflections and other properties from a real-world simulation.

Right below the lighting options, you will see another field called **Color**. There you can set the way your objects will appear in the 3D View. You can get:

- **Single**: Use a single color to display all objects equally. You can choose the tone at the selector below this button. The selector only appears if you select the **Single** option.
- **Material**: Shows objects with the same materials used in the **Material Editor**.
- **Random**: If you need greater understatement of a complex scene with dozens or hundreds of objects, you can use the random option to display a random color for each unique object. Blender will pick the colors for you.

At the bottom, you have another set of options, and from those options, you should take a close look at the **Shadow**. If you enable the **Shadow**, you will see a real-time shadow in your 3D View. The value next to the **Shadow** controls how dark they appear in your scene and with the little gears icon you can set the direction of your shadows.

By choosing **MatCap**, **Color** as **Random**, and enabling shadows, you will get the following view of your scene:

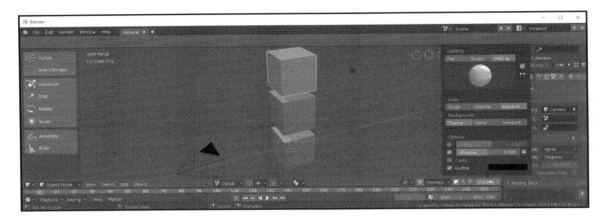

Figure 1.19: 3D View shading

You can change both **MatCap** and **Studio** shading options by clicking the preview sphere, as indicated in the next screenshot:

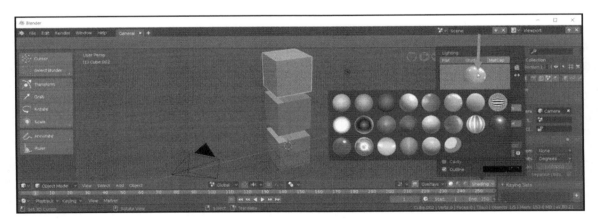

Figure 1.20: Changing the lights

Always use **MatCap** or **Studio** for projects that require a preview of volumetric shapes or during complex modeling tasks. They help you to become more productive.

Navigator widget and visualization

What if you have to manipulate the visualization of your objects in the 3D View of Blender? For that purpose, we can use the brand-new visualization options available in the user interface. Look at the top right corner of your 3D View, and there you will see five new icons that help controlling visualization, illustrated as follows:

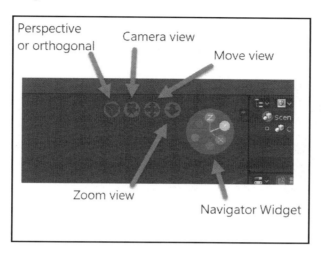

Figure 1.21: Navigation options

All those options will work with your mouse and are a great option with Blender, even if you don't have a mouse in your computer.

In the preceding diagram, you will find each of the following options:

- **Perspective or orthogonal**: The icon will enable you to swap between an orthogonal and perspective projection of lines for your 3D View. For modeling, tasks are always better to work with an orthogonal projection. You can also use the numpad *5* key as the shortcut for this option.
- **Camera view**: To quickly set the view to your active camera in Blender, you can click on this button. Click on it again to exit the camera view. The shortcut for this option is *Ctrl* + numpad *0*.
- **Move view**: Do you want to move the view? Click and drag in this icon to move your view and adjust the best possible angle. You can get the same results with the *Shift* + middle mouse button.

- **Zoom view**: To set zoom in and out you can click and drag the mouse up and down, to get a zoom in and out of your scene. Use the mouse wheel or + and - keys to get the same results.
- **Navigator widget**: A full navigation option for Blender.

Navigation widget

A navigation widget is a standard tool for 3D software, and Blender now has an option that allows you to orbit and adjust your visualization. One of the most simple choices for the widget is to rotate the visualization.

Click anywhere inside the circle icon with the right mouse button, and while you drag the cursor, you will rotate the visualization.

Notice that you will find the small circles inside the widget with the axis color codes. Some circles have a line connecting them to the center. Others are unconnected from the center.

What do they mean? Those are quick ways to set orthographical views. You can click at any circle to jump straight to a view. For instance, clicking the unconnected green circle will get you Front View. Using the connected green circle will give you the opposite, which is the Back View.

Here is a breakdown of all options from the navigation widget:

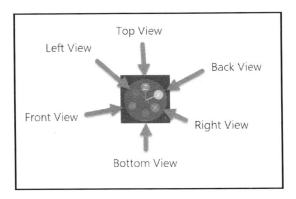

Figure 1.22: Navigation options

As with most of the options from the Blender user interface, you will find keyboard shortcuts for all views in the widget:

- **Top view**: numpad *3*
- **Bottom view**: *Ctrl* + numpad *3*
- **Front view**: numpad *1*
- **Back view**: *Ctrl* + numpad *1*
- **Right view**: numpad *7*
- **Left view**: *Ctrl* + numpad *7*

Displaying and editing properties

A useful option for any 3D tool like Blender is to give artists a way to see and edit object properties. Among those properties, you will find the location, rotation, and scale of those entities—the same properties that you already changed in the middle of this chapter.

What if you want to change those values using numeric precision?

Using the sidebar in Blender will give you access to those options and a little more! In the 3D View, to open the sidebar:

1. Press the *N* key shortcut or click at the small + icon at the top right corner, as indicated in the next screenshot:

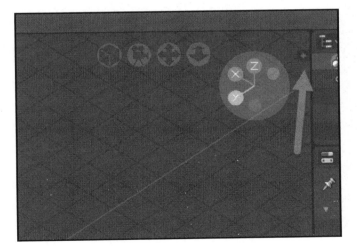

Figure 1.23: Sidebar icon

2. Once you click the icon, the sidebar will appear. To see properties for any given object, you must first select that object.

3. With the object selected, you will see numeric properties for **Location**, **Rotation**, and **Scale**, shown as follows:

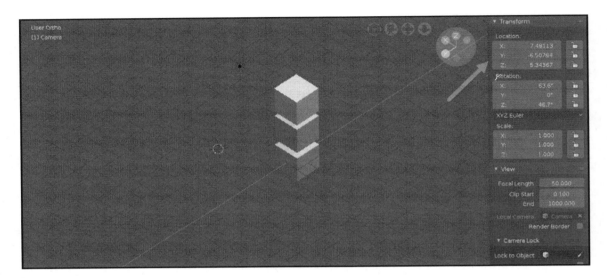

Figure 1.24: Sidebar options

4. To change the properties of the object, you can click at any numeric properties and set the desired value. For instance, you can set the object to have about half the size in the z axis setting the scale as 0.5 for the **Z** property, shown as follows:

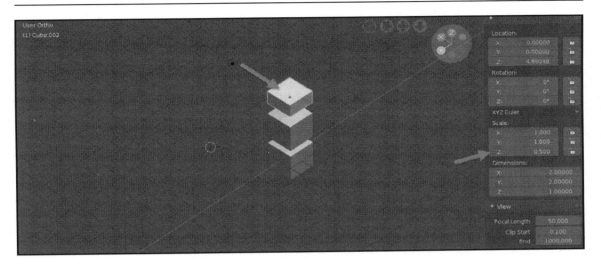

Figure 1.25: Setting the scale

You can also protect transformations for an object using the lock icons right next to each property.

 The 3D View is not the only window in Blender that will have a sidebar. You will find a similar option on several other window types. In the following chapters, you will see many more windows using the option to edit properties.

Summary

Understanding the user interface is critical to use Blender for any project, and now you have a solid knowledge of how to manipulate windows, transform 3D objects, change the zoom, and selection modes.

From this point, we can move to the next chapter and start to create 3D models from polygons, and also take advantage of the real-time rendering features of Eevee. There you will learn how to use tools like extrude and manage lights and shadows.

2
3D Modeling and Real-Time Rendering in Eevee

The first chapter of the book took a quick overview of the Blender user interface and some of the options available to manipulate windows and 3D visualization. From this point, we can start to create 3D content by using the 3D capabilities of Blender to create a 3D model and make a real-time render with Eevee.

Here is a list of what you will learn in this chapter:

- How to create 3D models in Blender
- Change the work mode to Edit
- Manage components from a polygon, such as vertices, edges, and faces
- Use extrusions to make models from 3D primitives
- Render a scene using Eevee and view real-time shadows

Technical requirements

You will be required to have Blender 2.80 installed to follow this procedure. Even if you have a later version of Blender, the described example should work with no significant problems.

The code files of this chapter can be found on GitHub:
`https://github.com/PacktPublishing/Blender-Quick-Start-Guide`.

Check out the following video to see the code in action:

`bit.ly/2R6Khis`.

Creating a chair model with polygons

What would software such as Blender be like, without powerful tools to create 3D models? In Blender, we have powerful tools that will give your imagination a blank canvas where you can create almost any project.

To show you the possibilities of 3D modeling with Blender, we will start a small project where you will create an object, and later add lights and effects in real time using Eevee.

At the end of this chapter, you will have a 3D model like the one shown in the following screenshot:

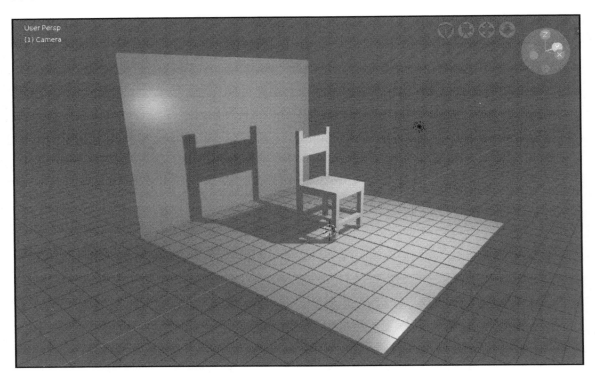

The technique used to create this chair is what artists call subdivision modeling. This technique means that we take a 3D primitive, such as a cube, and apply some deformation tools to turn it into a chair or any other object that you can imagine.

Starting with a 3D primitive

In the default startup scene from Blender, you will already find a cube primitive ready to use, as you probably remember from the last chapter. What if you don't have a cube, or your idea will work better by starting with another primitive, such as a sphere?

To create new 3D primitives in Blender, you can use the *Shift + A* shortcut, or the **Add** menu at the top of your user interface. In both options, you will get a menu that shows a list of possible alternatives you can create. For subdivision modeling, you should always pick primitives from the **Mesh** group.

But, for our example, we can start with a fresh Blender scene. You can open Blender and use the startup scene, or press the *Ctrl + N* keys to create a new blank file.

 If you have a model or scene that you want to save in Blender, you can always go to the **File** menu and choose **Save As...** to keep your work.

Creating the chair seat with transformations

Assuming that you now have a fresh startup scene in Blender with the default cube, we can begin our modeling project. The first thing to do is turn our cube into a chair seat. How do we do this? We will use a scale transformation.

Select the cube with a right-click and press the *S* key to apply a scale. Limit the scale to the Z-axis by pressing the *Z* key. You will notice that your cube will scale based on your mouse movement.

Before you click anywhere to confirm your transformation, we can use an option in Blender to set a precise value for that scale. Whenever you have an ongoing transformation in Blender, you can type numeric values in your keyboard to give it an accurate transformation.

On your keyboard, type 0.2 as the value and press *Enter*. That will confirm your scale.

 In Blender, all scale values work as proportional values. A scale of 1.0 is equal to 100% of the size of the object. A value of 0.2 will be 20% of the original size.

At the end of the process, you will have a cube that looks like the following screenshot:

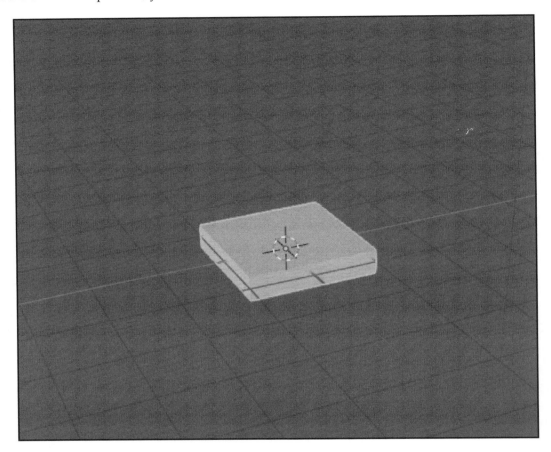

Expanding the chair with extrudes

The next step in our project is to take our cube and expand its sides to keep developing the basis for our chair. Until now, we have only worked with a mode in Blender called Object Mode. In that mode, you can only select and manipulate objects as a whole 3D mesh.

Every 3D mesh in Blender has three primary subcomponents that we can use to model:

- Vertices
- Edges
- Faces

How do we access those subcomponents? To see and manipulate them, we must change the work mode from Object to Edit. At the bottom of your 3D View, you can choose the work mode you want using the selector highlighted in the following screenshot:

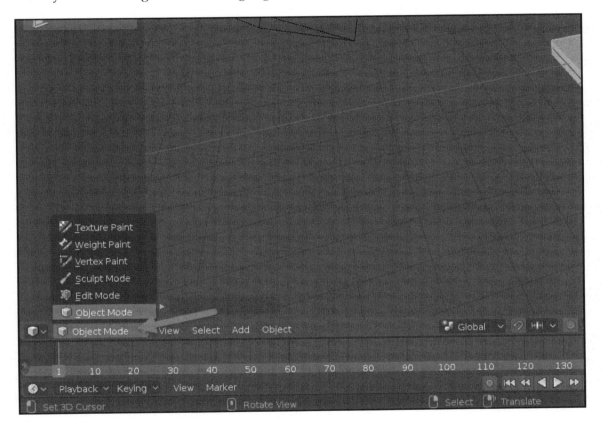

As you can see from this screenshot, you have several other work modes available, and they will change based on the object you have selected. For instance, if you choose a lamp, Blender won't show **Edit Mode** as an option. Lamps only have **Object Mode** available.

Once you change to **Edit Mode**, you will see a few different options in the 3D View. First, you will be able to select the object vertices. Look at the corners of your 3D model and you will see small dots that represent the vertices.

You can also select either edges or faces. For our project, you will work better with faces. Set the selection type to face using the option shown in the following screenshot, and select a single face from the side of your model:

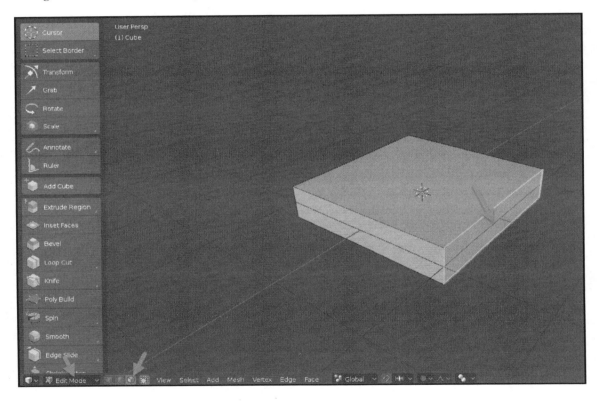

You can also change the selection type in **Edit Mode** using the *Ctrl + Tab* keys.

Blender has used a cube as the default scene for years, but it may change at any moment. If you don't see a cube as the starting object, you can always create a cube with the **Add** menu. Go to the Mesh group and pick **Cube**.

3D modeling with extrusions

Now that we have selected a single face of our 3D model, it is time to start using some powerful modeling tools. Have you ever heard of the extrude tool in 3D? That is one of the most used options to create polygonal models for all types of projects.

Blender has several options to create extrusions. If you paid attention to your Toolbar on the left, you may have noticed that a few options changed when you set the work mode to Edit.

In the Toolbar, you will see the three following options to work with extrudes:

- **Extrude Region**
- **Extrude Individual**
- **Extrude to cursor**

To see all three options, you have to click and hold with the left mouse button on the **Extrude Region** button. Notice the small triangle at the lower left corner of the button. That indicates it has additional options.

Most of the time you will only need the **Extrude Region** option. But what does an extrude actually do to the 3D model?

When you apply an extrude to a face, it will create a parallel copy of that same face, which will become connected on all sides to the surrounding edges of the original selection.

It sounds complicated, but it is incredibly easy to use.

Do you still have that face selected? Press the **Extrude Region** button, and you will see a big manipulator coming out of the face, as shown in the following screenshot:

You can now click and drag it at the + signs to start making an extrude. You can follow an axis with the respective color code, or use the yellow manipulator to make a perpendicular extrude. When you release the mouse button, you will have a new shape coming out of the selected face.

In our case, we will use the yellow manipulator. Click and drag the mouse while holding the *Ctrl* key to make an extrude. After you release the mouse button, you can change the distance used for the extrude with the floating menu in the 3D View. Set the value of the extrude to **0.25**, as shown in the following screenshot:

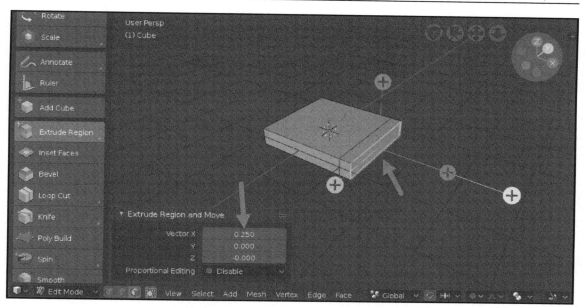

You can hold the *Ctrl* key while you drag the mouse in any transformation to use grid lines as a reference, and so gain better precision using the mouse.

Now, remove the face from the selection with the *Alt + A* key and apply the same extrude to the opposite side of your model. You will select the second face and apply the same process.

If you want to use a different approach, we can try a shortcut for extrusions, which is the *E* key.

After you select the face, press the *E* key and start moving the mouse to create the extrude. You must click somewhere to confirm the extrusion. But, before you click anywhere, you can type the value of that extrusion on your keyboard.

While you are still extruding, type 0.25 in your keyboard and press *Enter*. That will confirm the extrude with that length. In the end, you should have a model that looks like the following:

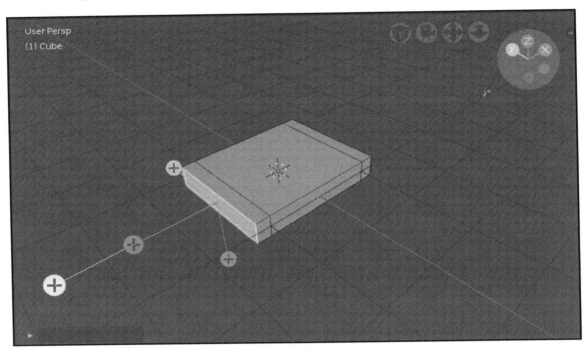

Something to bear in mind about numeric transformations and extrudes is the direction that you want to use. You may have to set the extrude with a negative value based on the direction in which your extrude is pointing. As a way to get the correct value, you can look at the status bar while you move your mouse.

It will show you the actual value of each extrude based on the direction you are using at the moment, as shown in the following screenshot. Another way to find the direction is with the transform widget. Following the same direction as the arrows will give you positive values, and the opposite direction will give negative ones.

You can cancel an extrude to start over at any moment (before you confirm it) with either a click, or *Enter* using the *Esc* key. But using *Esc* will only cancel the transformation; Blender will keep the geometry. Use *Ctrl + Z* to undo the operation entirely.

If you look around the 3D model that we have after those two extrudes, you will see that we have two sides that have only one large face covering each whole side, and two other sides that have three faces each. We will work with the sides that have three faces.

It is time to use the **Extrude Individual** option to save some time with our 3D modeling. What you have to do now is select all six faces from both opposing sides of the model. You can hold the *Shift* key and right-click on each of them to select them.

After you have all those faces selected, press and hold the **Extrude Individual** button, as seen in the following screenshot:

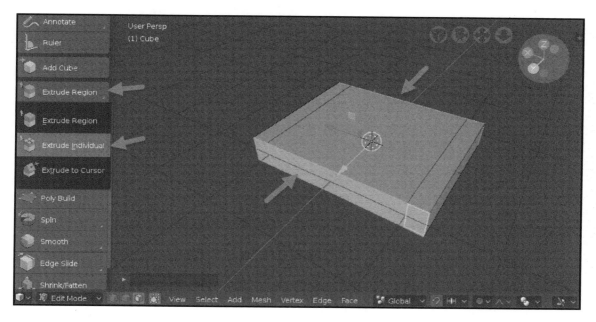

Extrude Individual will apply the same type of extruding as we used in the Region option, but to multiple faces at once. If you click and drag the faces, you will notice that they will expand in opposite directions.

Click anywhere to confirm the extrude and, using the same floating menu, set the size to -0.25, as shown in the following screenshot:

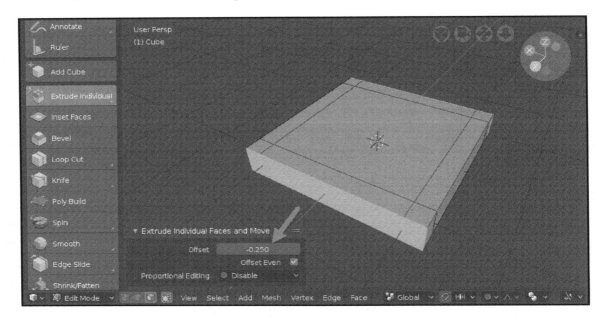

Is there a shortcut for **Extrude Individual**? Absolutely! You can do the same procedure using the *Alt + E* keys and by typing the value of the extrude as -0.25.

Creating the legs and the Specials menu

Why did we apply all those extrudes to the sides of our 3D model? The reason for so many extrudes is so that, at the end, we have four small planes at the sides of our seat. Using those planes, we will be able to use additional extrudes as a way to quickly create all the other parts of our chair.

Do you want to see how easy it is will be to create the legs for the chair?

If you rotate the model using either the Navigation Widget or the middle mouse button, you will be able to move the view to the bottom of your seat. At this point, you should select all four small faces in the corners of the model.

TIP

To select multiple objects, you can hold the *Shift* key and right-click on each face.

With that faces selected, you should apply three consecutive extrudes with values of 1.3, 0.2, and 0.5. You can use the **Extrude Region** button for this, or use the *E* key and then type in the values as before. Why not negative values? In the **Extrude Region**, we use positive values to go toward the normals of a face. Imagine a perpendicular coming out of each face.

In the end, you will have something like the following:

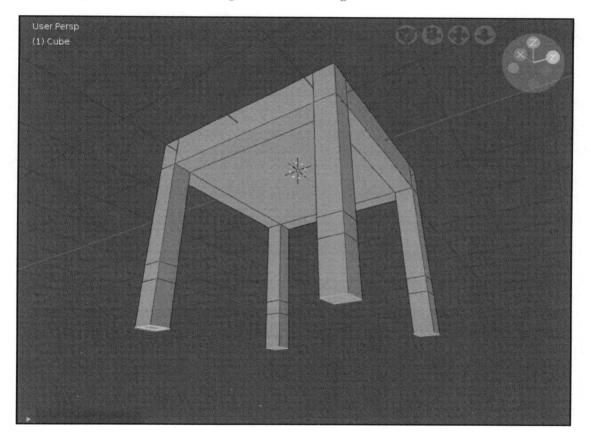

Is there a reason for applying three extrudes? If you go back to the very first screenshot in this chapter, you will see that our chair legs have connections between them. Using three extrudes will create the necessary segments that we can use later to create connections between the legs quickly, without the need for any further modeling.

To create the connections, we will use the Specials menu in Blender. The menu only appears in **Edit Mode**, and you can activate it using the *W* key.

Select two of the small faces, with 0.2 in height, on opposite sides of the chair. Press the *W* key to open the Specials menu and choose **Bridge Faces**. Using that option will connect two parallel faces, as shown in this screenshot:

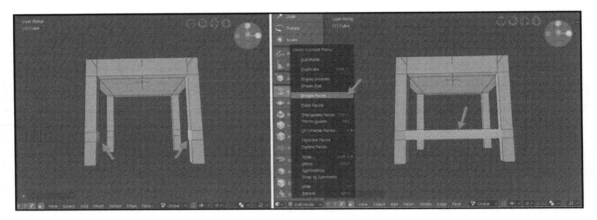

Repeat the same process for all other sides of the chair, until you have something that looks like the following:

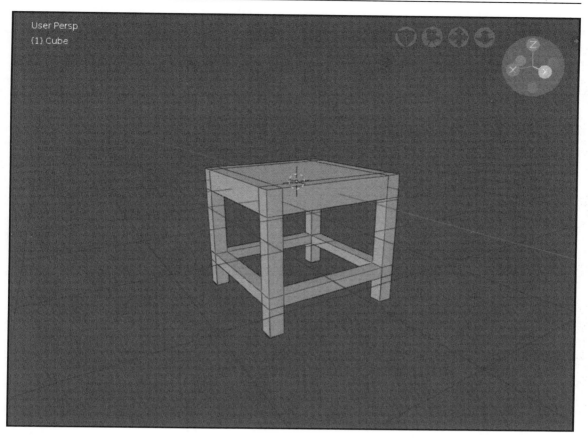

Bridge Faces is a simple yet powerful way to create 3D models in Blender.

Creating the backrest

In 3D modeling, you will notice that you can apply the same principles and tools to create different shapes and objects. We just created the legs of our chair and, using the same tools and procedures, we can make the backrest.

Using the orbit tools in Blender, you can set the view to see our model from the top. From that angle, you can quickly select only two faces at the top of our chair. Select two faces on the same side.

Apply three extrudes to those two faces, with lengths of 1.5, 0.9, and 0.4 respectively. You can use extrude region for those extrudes, as shown in the following screenshot:

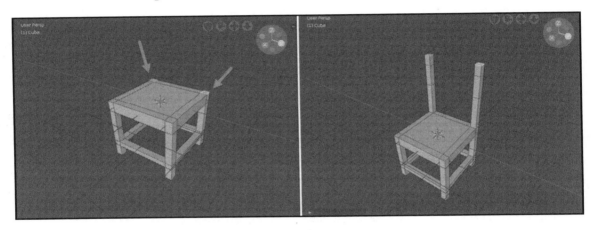

Why three extrudes? For the same reason that we used them for the legs—to create a reference in our model and quickly create the backrest.

Now, select the two opposite faces pointing to the middle point of your recently extruded shape. Press the *W* key and choose **Bridge Faces** again. By the end, you will have a backrest just like the following screenshot:

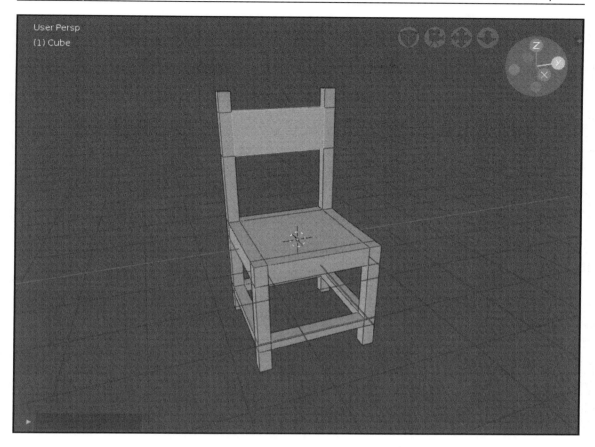

Using pie menus in Blender 2.8

Among the new features of Blender 2.8, pie menus, offer a quick way to change modes and pick selection types in the program. An essential aspect of pie menus is that it is an **Add-on** for Blender. What is an **Add-on**?

This is something like a plugin for Blender, written in Python. With an **Add-on**, you can easily choose whether you want it as part of Blender or not. All add-ons in Blender have a control panel where you can enable and disable them.

To open that panel you have to use the Edit menu and choose **User Preferences...**.

There you will use a tab called **Add-ons,** and from the list on the left, you can pick the category of a particular add-on that you want to control. What if you don't know the location of an add-on? Just type the name into the search box and Blender will list them for you. Enable the **Pie Menu: UI Pie Menu Official**.

Right below the pie menu add-on controls, you can see a list with all shortcuts that can be used with pie menus.

So how do we use them?

Simple—once you are in Object Mode, press the *Tab* key and you will see a pie menu with a list of options offering you different modes to pick. Choose the mode you want, and Blender will set that for your object, as shown in the following screenshot:

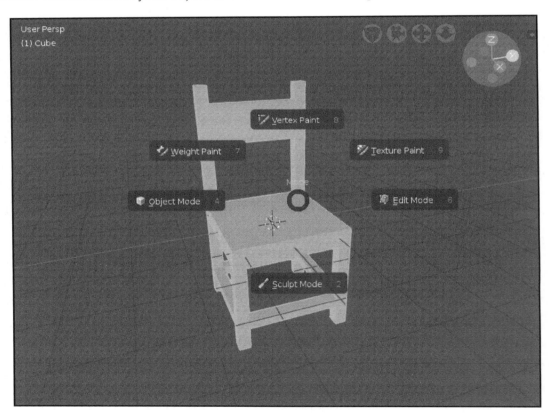

What happens if you don't use pie menus? Before Blender 2.8, using the *Tab* key alone, without the pie menus add-on, would swap between Object and **Edit Mode**. By disabling pie menus, you can bring this behavior back to version 2.8.

However, using pie menus does have several advantages, such as offering shortcuts to other options:

- **Transformation mode**: Toggle between **Translation**, **Rotation**, and **Scaling** transformations using the *Ctrl* + Space bar keys.
- **Shade mode**: With the *Z* key, you can see options related to shading for 3D models. You can either smooth or flatten their surfaces.
- **Pivot menu**: Use the . key to view a list of possible places to set the pivot point for your 3D model.
- **Toggle snap**: To quickly turn on snapping for modeling, you can use the *Ctrl* + *Shift* + *Tab* keys to call a pie menu.
- **View options**: A lot of options related to viewing in Blender will appear in a pie menu that you can trigger with the *Q* key. For instance, you can swap between a perspective and orthogonal projection.

 How do you close a pie menu? You can always close the menu using the *Esc* key if you don't want to use it anymore.

From this point forward, you should use pie menus for all your interactions with Blender.

Adding a floor and back wall

It is now time to add another part of your scene, so that we can start rendering with Eevee. If you plan to create a scene where the objects will cast shadows, you need a surface to receive shadows. Using just a floating chair in a 3D landscape will give us only a limited capability to show shadows.

For that reason, we will add a floor and a back wall to the scene.

Make sure you are in Object Mode and then press the *Shift* + *A* key. Choose the **Plane** option in the **Mesh** group. Using this option will add a plane to your scene.

With the plane selected, move the object until it is below your chair. Don't worry if it doesn't stay precisely below. We will fix that later. The plane will probably require a scale transformation. Use the *S* key to make it a lot bigger—something like four or five times bigger.

Now, press the *Tab* key and set the mode to Edit.

In **Edit Mode**, select the edge of your plane that is in the back of your chair. You can either choose one edge or two vertices. That will depend on the selection type you have at the moment.

With that edge selected, you can either press the *E* key and then the *Z* key to extrude, or use the Extrude Region button on the left, as shown in the following screenshot:

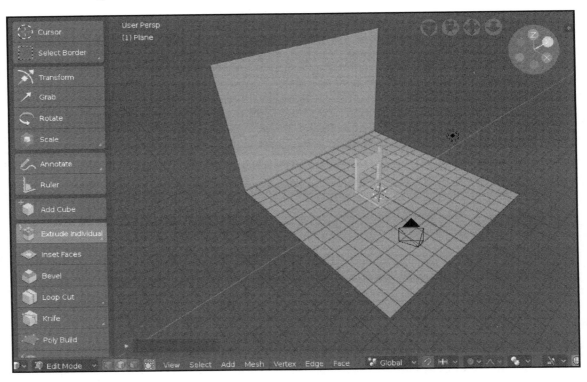

 You can also set the extrude using the space bar to open a floating menu with all options from the Toolbar.

As you can see from the previous screenshot, we now have the floor and back wall for the chair. This was the same technique used to build the chair, and you can replicate it in several ways to create other objects. Go to Object mode and try to place the chair on top of the floor plane.

Rendering and shading with Eevee

In Blender 2.8, we have a brand new and revolutionary render engine called Eevee. One of the most significant advantages of Eevee is the possibility to create and visualize realistic renders in real time. Although you can create realistic renders in Blender using Cycles, this will require several minutes or hours to process, whereas Eevee will give you instantaneous results.

How do we start with Eevee? The first thing to do is to set your 3D View to display all objects in render mode. You can do that using the three small buttons close to the Shading options, as shown in the following screenshot:

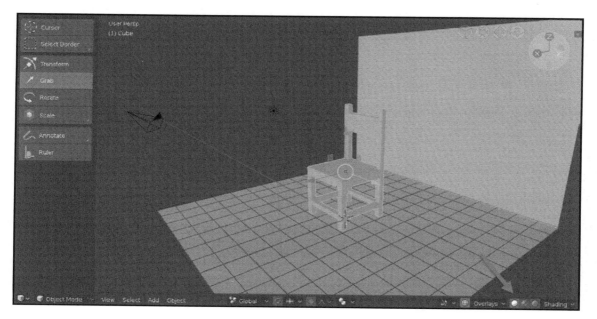

Use the last button on the right to set your view to Render. That will trigger Render mode, and you will start to see shadows, highlights, and other details, as shown in the following screenshot:

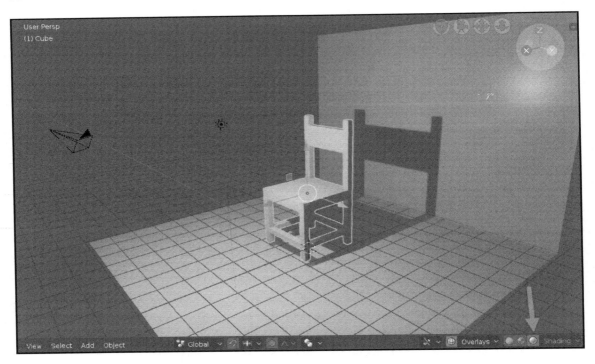

Do you want to make sure Eevee is your render engine? Open the Render tab in the properties window, and at the top you will see a selector for your render engine. If Eevee is not selected, you can change your render engine in this panel:

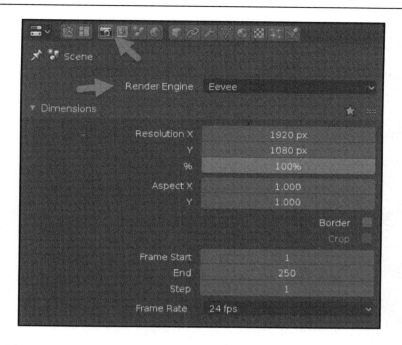

 Almost all options related to Eevee will also work with Cycles. However, Cycles will require you to process the scene to see realistic results. Renders in Cycles will look better, but in most cases you can achieve great renders in Eevee.

Adding lights and real-time shadows

Depending on the position of your lamp in Blender, you will start to see shadows in the scene at the exact moment you set the view to rendered. Since Eevee uses a real-time display of shadows; you can select the lamp in the scene and move it around to see updates to the shadow position.

Changing light types and strength

With the lamp still selected, you can open the Object Data tab in the properties window in Blender to see all options related to lights. At the top, you can change your light type and set values for color and energy.

The first option will set the color that your light will emit, and the second, specifies how intense your light will be, as shown:

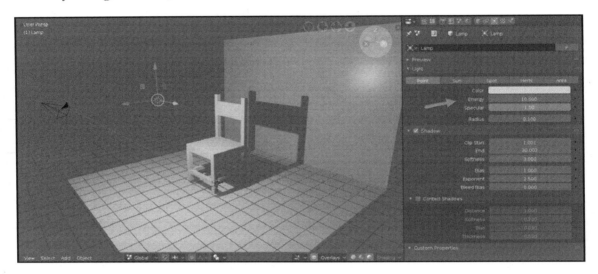

 The Object Data tab changes based on context. For instance, when you select a lamp, it will display options for that object type. If you choose a 3D model, it will show options related to that object.

Shadow quality

At the bottom of the Object Data tab, you will see essential settings for shadows, as shown in the following screenshot. The first group of options give you the ability to enable or disable shadows with a **Shadow** group. By default, this option will always start enabled.

In the second group, you will find **Contact shadows**, which will create an additional shadow below your objects. A contact shadow will only appear when two surfaces are close to each other. Use this option to increase realism in your projects:

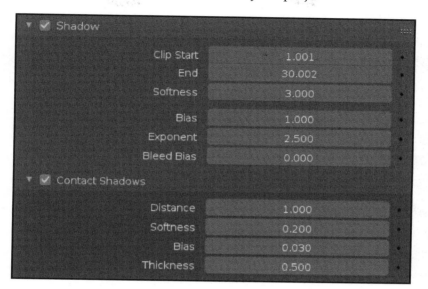

By default, you have to turn on contact shadows on each light. Besides being a great tool to enhance realism, using too many contact shadows may start to delay the rendering of your results. When you change your view using the zoom controls, Blender might need additional seconds to recalculate shadows.

That was just an overview of how you can start rendering and controlling lights, and how to render in Eevee. In Chapter 6, *Lights and Real-Time Rendering with Blender Eevee*, we will get back to lights and rendering.

Rendering still images

We now have a scene that has lights and real-time shadows, and we can render that into a still image. The first thing you have to know about rendering is that Blender only renders the view from our active camera.

To set your view to the active camera, you can use the small camera icon at the top right of your 3D View, highlighted in the following screenshot, or use the 0 key on the numpad. If you want to exit this view, you can either click on the camera icon again, or use the middle mouse button to orbit the scene:

How do you change what your active camera is seeing at the moment?

The easiest way to adjust the viewing angle of your active camera is with the zoom controls. Set the 3D View zoom as you want and press the *Ctrl + Alt +* numpad *0* keys.

Using this magical shortcut will make your active camera align with the current view of your scene.

If you still need some adjustment, select the camera frame border, as highlighted in the following screenshot, and then, using the *G* key, you can move your camera to the sides. To make a dolly movement, you will need to move your camera along the local *Z*-axis by pressing the *G* key and *Z* key twice:

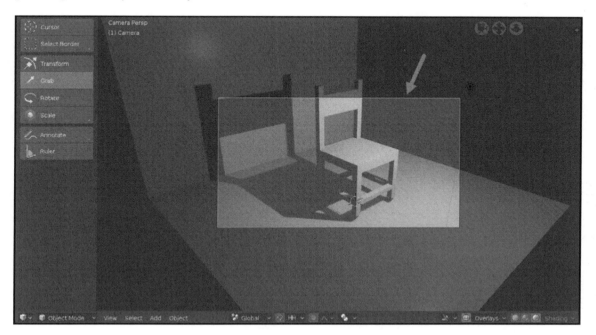

Rendering with Eevee

Rendering in Blender is incredibly easy—you can trigger this task by using the *F12* key on your keyboard, or with the Render menu. In the render menu, you can choose **Render Image**.

That will start the rendering, and display the results of your scene, which should look something like the following:

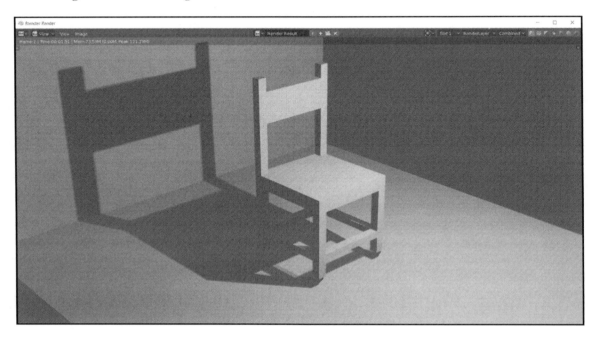

You can save the render in the Image menu by using the **Save As...** option.

How do you set the size of your render image? At the top of the render tab, you will see a field called `Dimensions`. There you can choose the width and height of your render images, as shown in the following screenshot:

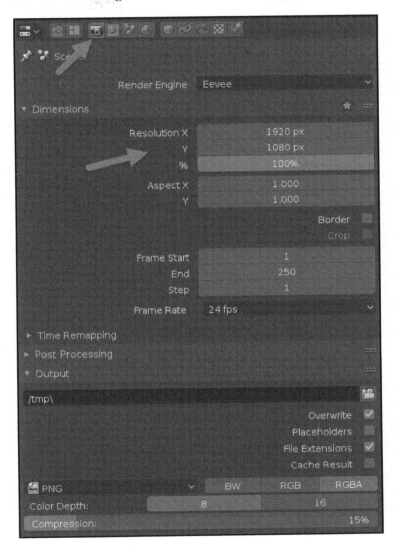

Summary

Having a 3D scene like the one you just created in this chapter will help you apply and experiment with other options in Blender, both in terms of modeling and rendering. Save the scene for use with the following chapters in this book.

The next chapter will introduce more options regarding modeling, such as the 3D Cursor and modifiers.

3
The New 3D Cursor and Modeling Options

Blender has a significant number of tools for 3D modeling and object manipulation, such as the 3D Cursor. Up to now, we have only used some of those tools to create a scene in both Chapter 1, *Using Blender 2.8 UI, Shading and Navigator Widget*, and Chapter 2, *3D Modeling and Real-Time Render in Eevee*. It is now time to see how you can use options such as the 3D Cursor to align and gain additional controls for your Blender projects.

The following is what you will learn in this chapter:

- Use and manipulate the 3D Cursor
- Cut models
- Use modifiers
- Align objects with additional snap tools

Technical requirements

You will be required to have Blender 2.80 installed to follow this procedure. Even if you have a later version of Blender, the described example should work with no significant problems.

The code files of this chapter can be found on GitHub:
https://github.com/PacktPublishing/Blender-Quick-Start-Guide.

Check out the following video to see the code in action:

bit.ly/2N6CLkw.

Using the 3D Cursor

The 3D Cursor is a feature of Blender that usually causes some confusion among artists with no prior experience of the software. No other 3D tool has anything that looks like the 3D Cursor, but they should consider adopting a similar solution.

Where is the 3D Cursor? If you take a close look at the 3D View window, you will find a little crosshair icon, which is the 3D Cursor, shown as follows:

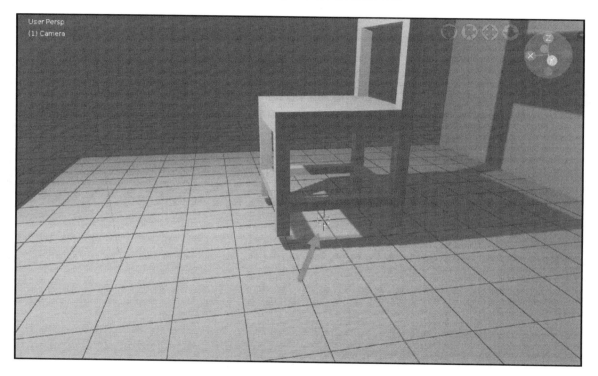

Figure 3.1: The 3D Cursor

In Blender, the 3D Cursor is a helper that will mainly give you a visual reference for the following:

- Creating objects
- Aligning objects
- Working as a temporary pivot point
- Setting origin points for objects

Whenever you create a new object in Blender, it will appear at the 3D View at the exact location of the 3D Cursor.

You can click and drag the 3D Cursor at any object surface, and Blender will try to align the orientation of the cursor with the surface automatically.

For instance, you can add another object to the scene and it will appear at the location of your 3D Cursor. To set the position of the cursor, you can left-click anywhere in the 3D View, which will place the cursor with little precision.

If you want to reset the position of the 3D Cursor at any time, use the View menu at the bottom of your 3D View, and choose **Align View** | **Center Cursor** and **View All**.

Using the cursor to align objects

To demonstrate the power of the 3D Cursor, we can use it to place the chair model, created in the previous chapter, precisely on the floor.

In Blender, an origin point for objects is the reference location used to determine location and pivot points for both rotation and scale.

1. The first step is to set the origin point for the model, on the legs' lower faces.
2. Select the chair model and change the mode to Edit. In Edit Mode, select only the lower faces of the chair legs. You can use the *B* key to make a border selection.

3. With the faces selected, we can align the 3D Cursor with the selected objects. To do that, Blender has a snap tool. Press the *Shift + S* key and the snap tools will appear. Choose the **Cursor to Selected**, shown as follows:

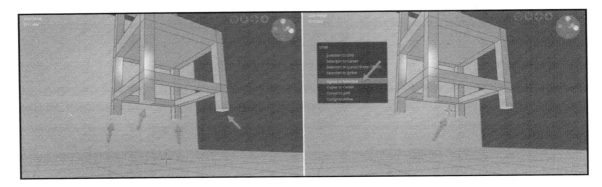

Figure 3.2: Aligning the cursor

4. Using the snap with the **Cursor to Selected** will move the cursor to the central location of any selected objects. Now, go to Object Mode, and in the Object Menu you can choose **Transform | Origin to 3D Cursor**, shown as follows:

Figure 3.3: Origin to 3D cursor

5. That will move the origin point of any selected object to the 3D Cursor location. You will notice the small dot representing the origin at the same position as the cursor.

6. With the origin point of the chair set, we can now select the other object representing the floor and wall. Go to Edit mode and select only the face representing the floor. Use *Shift + S* again and choose, once again, the **Cursor to Selected** option, shown as follows:

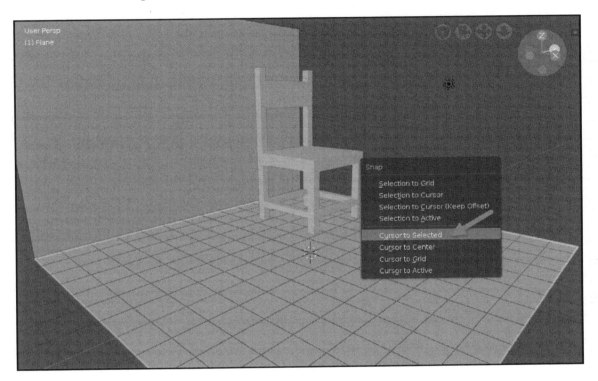

Figure 3.4: Cursor to the floor

Both the floor and wall form a single object. You can split objects into separate entities using the *P* key. In Edit Mode, select an object and press the *P* key. Choose **Selected**, and Blender will get the chosen parts and create a new object.

7. Now we have a perfect situation to use our cursor to align the chair with the floor.

Select the chair model in Object Mode, and press the *Shift + S* keys. Choose the **Selected to Cursor** option, and Blender will move the chair to the current location of our 3D Cursor, as shown in the following screenshot. Since the cursor is at the same position as the floor, we will have the chair precisely aligned with the object:

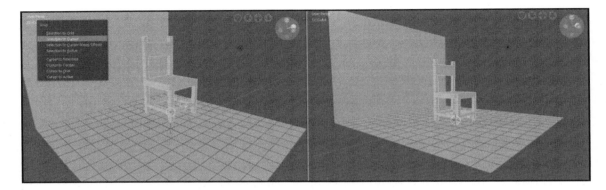

Figure 3.5: Align the chair

You can always use the 3D Cursor as a starting point for modeling, which will save a significant amount of time in your projects. Together with the snap tool, you have a powerful yet simple way to add objects to your projects with precision.

3D Cursor coordinates and display

Sometimes you may want to have precise control over the 3D Cursor location, for example, having it at a particular coordinate. You can change the numeric values of the cursor location using the properties tab, as in the following screen shot.

At the properties options, you can change the cursor coordinates. To open the properties tab, you can use the *N* key in the 3D View:

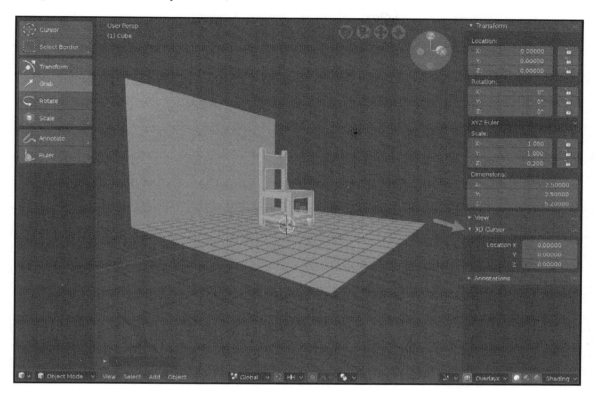

Figure 3.6: 3D Cursor options

Cutting the model

The wall model is only a large plane at the back of our scene. We can make it a lot more interesting by adding a door. For that, we will cut the model using a tool in Blender called Loop Cut. The *Ctrl + R* keys are a shortcut for loop cuts, but they only work in **Edit Mode**.

There is also a dedicated button on the Toolbar, as follows:

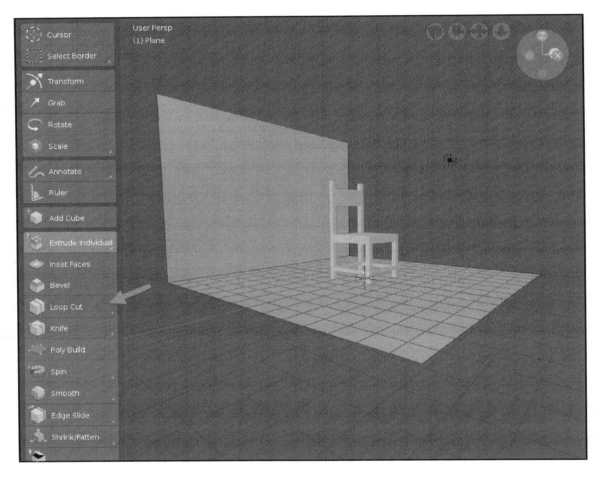

Figure 3.7: Loop Cut button

When you trigger the loop cut, you will have to use your mouse cursor to choose an edge to cut. The cut will be perpendicular to the edge. With a click, you can set the direction of the cut, and Blender will ask you for the location of the cut.

Once you choose a direction, you will be able to move your mouse to pick a location for the cut. Use a second click to set the cut location.

In short, you will just need two clicks, one to pick a direction and another to set a location for the cut.

 The technical name of a series of connected edges is an edge loop. For that reason, you will find the name loop cut.

Creating a doorway and modifiers

To create a doorway, we can select the wall model and use the *Ctrl + R* keys or the **Toolbar** button, to activate the loop cut. Remember, you have to click twice to first set the direction of the cut and then to choose a position for the new loops.

Here are the steps to cut:

1. Press the *Ctrl + R* keys or use the Toolbar button.
2. Move the mouse over the edge you want to cut and left-click once to choose the cut direction.
3. Now you will select the cut position. Move the mouse and left-click again to mark the cut location.

For the door at the back of your model, you will need two cuts. Make the first one as shown in the following left screenshot, and the second as shown in the following right screenshot:

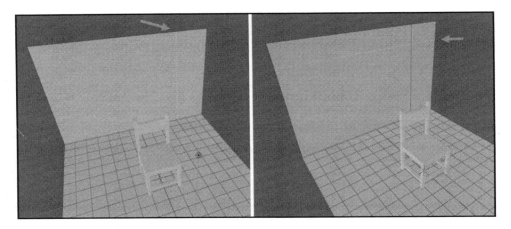

Figure 3.8: Making two cuts

The next step is to select the large face at the lower-right corner of the wall and extrude it backward (*E* key). After you finish the extrude, erase the three faces indicated in the following screenshot with the *Delete* or *X* key:

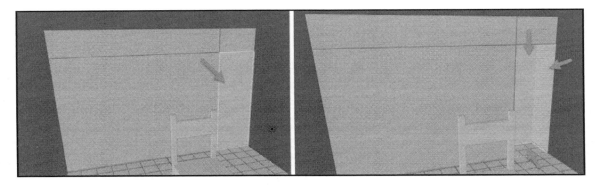

Figure 3.9: Extruding the wall

As you can see in the previous screenshot, we will have an incredibly narrow hole for the door because it is half the width of a regular door.

We will use a modifier to copy and mirror the geometry in Blender to the other site. What is a modifier? It is a unique option in Blender that you can apply to objects for modeling, animation, and effects.

You can add multiple modifiers to the same object, stack them in order, and eventually apply them to the objects.

To add a modifier, you have to use the modifiers panel in the properties window. For our wall, we will use the mirror modifier, as shown in the following screenshot:

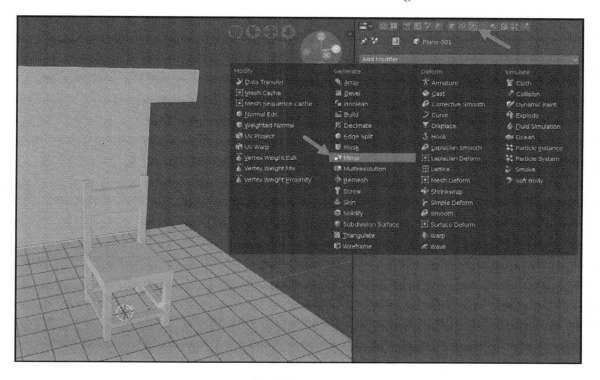

Figure 3.10: Mirror modifier

Before you add the mirror modifier, we have to set the pivot point for the mirror. The mirror modifier will create a mirrored copy of your 3D model, using the origin point as a pivot. For that reason, we have to set the origin point of the object, as shown in the following screenshot:

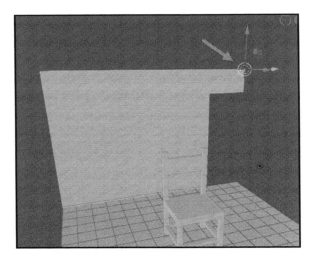

Figure 3.11: The Pivot point

You can use the 3D cursor to get the exact point for the pivot.

With the origin point in place, add the mirror modifier and choose the correct axis for the mirror. In our case, it will be the Y-axis, a shown in the following screenshot:

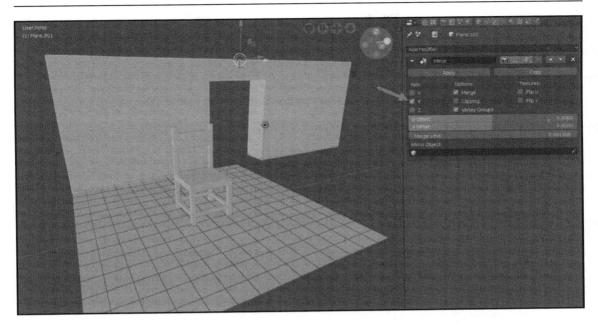

Figure 3.12: Adding the mirror

Repeat the same process for the floor model, and you will have a full mirror of the scene.

Snap during transformations

Even with a tool such as the 3D Cursor that helps with alignment, you still can get another great option to place objects using reference points such as vertices, edges, and faces.

In the Blender user interface, you will find a small magnet icon at the bottom of your 3D View window, which will activate the snap during a transformation action. Once you enable the tool, all transformations will start to look for reference points.

For instance, when you move objects, Blender will start to look for vertices that are close to each other. Once it finds a vertex that matches your criteria, Blender will place them together.

Where is this tool? You will find it at the bottom of the 3D View window as a small magnet icon, as indicated in the following screenshot. You can also enable and disable the tool with the *Shift + Tab* keys. Click at the button right next to the magnet to set the options for snapping:

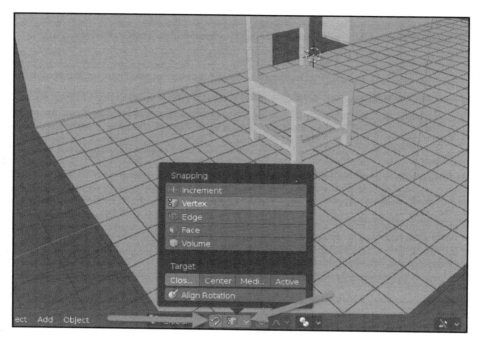

Figure 3.13: Snap icon

You have to choose a snapping element and then a target. The element will set what Blender will look to position an object. The options are increment (grid lines), vertex, edge, face, and volume (whole object). For the target, you have to choose what parameter Blender must use to track both objects. As targets for snap, you can pick closest, center, median, and active.

For instance, you can set the snapping to vertex and target to closest, and by selecting and moving the chair, it will quickly snap to the wall.

To achieve that, you have first to select the chair and activate the snap. Choose the proper element and target. Place the mouse cursor near the location you wish to snap to and press the *G* key, as shown in the following screenshot:

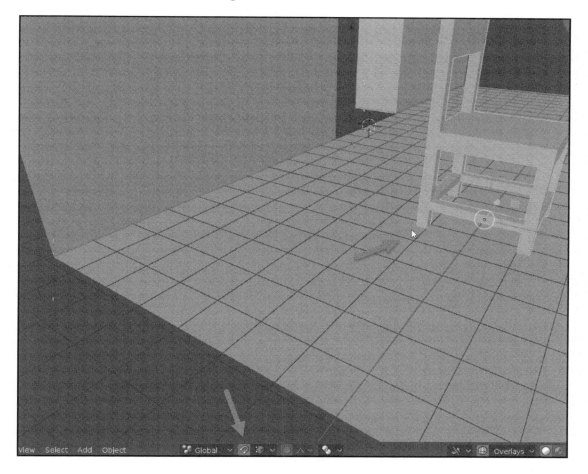

Figure 3.14: Snap preparations

Now, move the mouse until you reach a corner of the wall. A small circle will appear near the vertex that Blender will capture as the closest vertex to the object. If you click there, your model will stay at that location using only the mouse, as shown in the following screenshot:

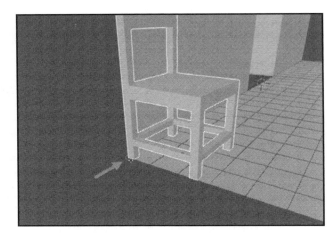

Figure 3.15: Placing the object

With the snap during transform, you can have full control over locations using only the mouse.

Another great feature of that tool is the **Align Rotation** option, which can spin and align your objects with non orthogonal surfaces, as shown in the following screenshot:

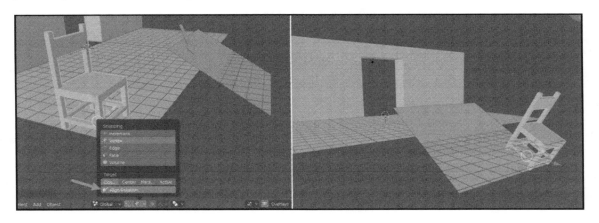

Figure 3.16: Align Rotation

Summary

Using modeling tools in Blender will give you more creative freedom to create almost any type of object in 3D. In this last chapter, you learned how to use some of the most commonly used modeling tools for precise transformations, such as snapping, and also modifiers.

Modifiers are a powerful resource for any modeling project and will help you in object duplication (array modifier), polygon smoothing (subdivision surface modifier), and much more.

The next chapter will introduce materials in Blender and how we can boost realism for our models by adding meaning to surfaces. For instance, we will add a simple color to objects and other effects, such as reflections.

4
Using Real-Time Materials in Eevee

Materials are a powerful way to add context to any scene in 3D, and Blender has a wide range of options to combine and create materials. In the following chapter, you will find all the information necessary to create and use materials in Eevee.

In addition, you will also find a brand-new tool in Blender that we haven't used until now. The Shader Editor is a unique area in the Blender user interface for crafting and setting materials using nodes.

Here is a list of what you will learn:

- How to create materials
- Select shaders
- Set material color
- Add reflections to surfaces
- Create transparency effects
- Use multiple materials in the same object

Technical requirements

You will be required to have Blender 2.80 installed to follow this procedure. Even if you have a later version of Blender, the described example should work with no significant problems.

The code files of this chapter can be found on GitHub:
https://github.com/PacktPublishing/Blender-Quick-Start-Guide.

Check out the following video to see the code in action:

`bit.ly/2NJaF3T.`

Using materials in Blender

A material in 3D softwares such as Blender will help you identify the nature of a surface and how it reacts to light. It will help determine whether a surface must reflect, absorb, or scatter light.

To create materials in Blender, you will have two main options:

- The **Materials** tab in the properties window: For basic material options such as assigning a color or setting reflections, the properties window will work fine.
- The shader editor: Once you need more complex and refined materials, you will have to use the shader editor.

Since Eevee is a real-time render engine, it will give you instant visual feedback on all materials you create and assign in Blender. All you have to do is set the Shader as rendered, and you will see the results in the 3D View window.

Adding materials to objects

Blender has a simple rule regarding materials that you may want to remember, which is that any material must have an object associated. What happens if you don't follow that rule? If Blender finds a material that doesn't have an object, it will purge the material from your file.

What if you want to keep a material with no object assigned? For that, you will find something called Fake User to protect materials from a possible exclusion.

Before we take a look at the Fake User controls, let's see where to set up and configure materials. You will find the controls on the **Materials** tab in the properties window. Select an object, such as our chair, and open the **Materials** tab.

 The Fake User is present for more data types in Blender and not only materials. You will find the same **F** icon for textures, 3D objects, and more.

You may see an empty panel if your object doesn't have any materials. In this case, you can either click the **New** button to create an empty material or use the button on the left and pick an existing material from your file, as denoted by the red arrows in the following screenshot:

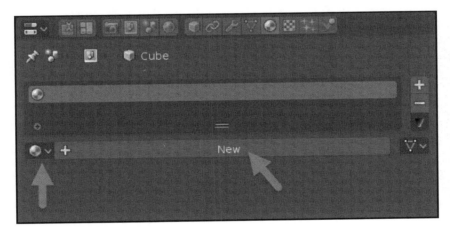

Figure 4.1: Material creation

Once you create a material, you will see more controls to set all visual properties of your surfaces. In the following screenshot, you will see a breakdown of the controls:

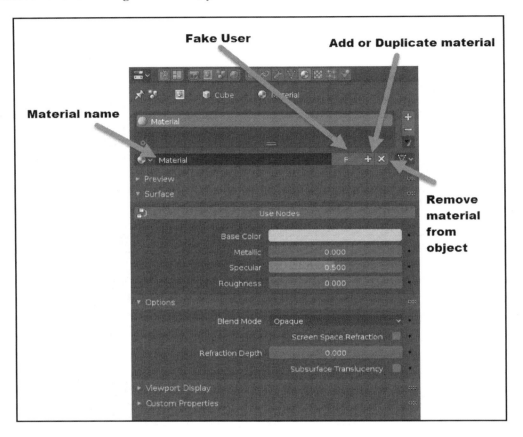

Figure 4.2: Material options

What about the Fake User? If you want to protect the material, click on the **F** button and you will preserve the content.

Notice that you also have a button called **Use Nodes**. When this button appears, it means you don't have shaders associated with the material. In this case, you should press the button to display advanced shader options.

 You should always assign unique names to your materials in Blender to better navigate and edit your scenes in the future.

Using shaders for materials

Before we proceed, it will be wise to enable a feature of Eevee for rendering to better display real results in the 3D View window. Go to the render panel and enable **Screen Space Reflections**, as shown in the next screenshot:

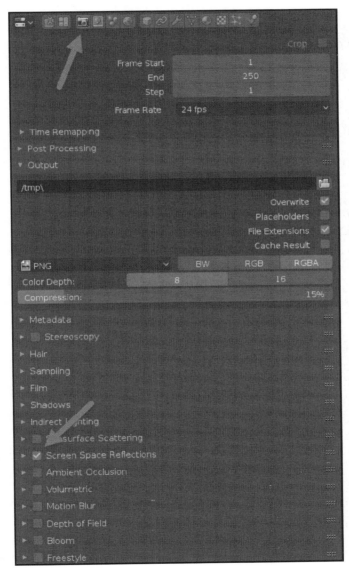

Figure 4.3: Screen space reflections

When this option is in use, Blender will show reflections and other advanced properties of materials. From this point forward, you must set the shading of your 3D View as rendered for a real-time preview of materials.

By the time you turn on Nodes for materials, Blender will show a powerful shader called **Principled BSDF**. A shader is responsible for telling the software how light will interact with a surface, as shown in the following screenshot:

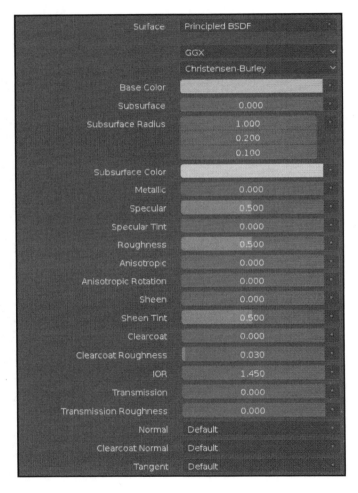

Figure 4.4: Principled BSDF

What does the **BSDF** acronym mean? It is short for **Bidirectional Scattering Distribution Function**, which is the mathematical function describing how light interacts with a surface.

With the **Principled BSDF**, you can set properties of surfaces such as reflections, color, and much more. We will also use the shader in `Chapter 5`, *Real-Time Textures for Eevee*, to configure textures.

Are there any more shaders in Blender? Yes, you will find a lot more shaders.

Other shaders will show far fewer options than the **Principled BSDF**, and in a lot of cases, you might get faster results with more straightforward choices. To change the shader type, you can click on the **Principled BSDF** name to see all options.

We will use the **Principled BSDF** shader mainly to create PBR materials using multiple textures in
`Chapter 5`, *Real-Time Textures for Eevee.*

Object color

The simplest option for materials in Blender is to assign a color to an object. For that type of property, you can use the **Diffuse BSDF** shader. Choosing the **Diffuse BSDF** will give you the choice of picking a color and setting a roughness for the surface.

For instance, if we select the chair model and, with a material assigned to the object, click the color selector, and you can pick another color tone. You will see an immediate change in the object color, as shown in the following screenshot:

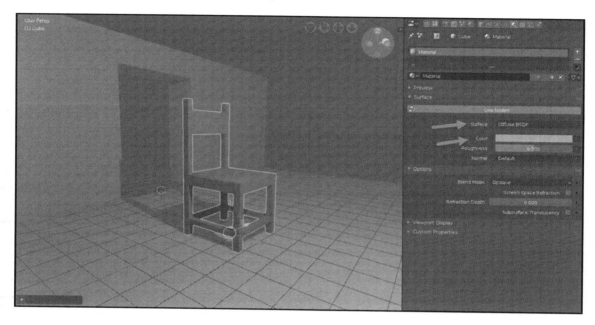

Figure 4.5: Object color

Reflections for materials

The next main characteristic of a material that you will want to look at is reflection. In Blender, you can get full control over reflections with the **Glossy BSDF** shader.

For instance, select the floor object of our scene and add a new material. Select the material shader as **Glossy BSDF**, and you will see the same color picker and roughness from the **Diffuse BSDF**. But here, the roughness will control the behavior of your reflections.

A value of zero for the roughness will create a perfect mirror; anything higher than zero will start to blur the reflection. The maximum value will result in a blurred reflection, as shown in the next screenshot:

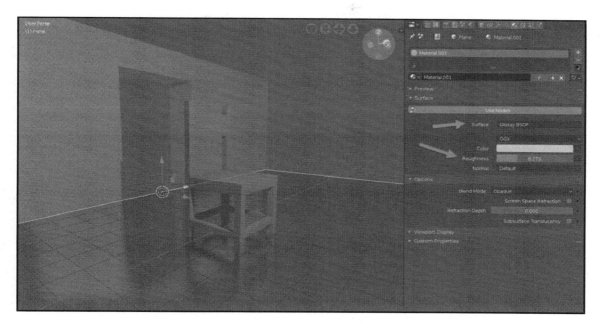

Figure 4.6: Reflections with the Glossy BSDF

Transparency for materials

Another type of property for materials that you will probably want to use in your projects is transparency. How do we create transparent materials? Before we go further, showing shaders for transparent materials, it is important to state something about transparency.

At the moment, Eevee won't display real-time transparency on your 3D View. You will have to swap renders to **Cycles**.

To change your render, you can go to the Render panel and in the **Render Engine** choose **Cycles**, as shown in the following screenshot:

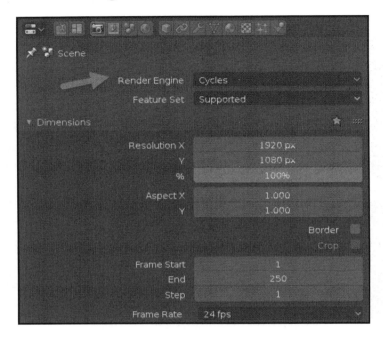

Figure 4.7: Changing the renderer

Once you change to **Cycles** and keep your 3D View shading as rendered, you will notice that Blender will use progressive rendering to display the results. The scene starts rendering with a lot of noise, and it will progressively remove the noise.

If you want to see how to control the quality of your render, go to Chapter 6, *Lights and Real-Time Rendering with Blender Eevee*, to see a description of **Cycles** controls.

With **Cycles** selected, we can go back to our materials. Add a sphere to the scene to better see your transparency and place it between your camera and the chair model.

Add a material to the sphere and choose the shader as **Transparent BSDF**, as shown in the next screenshot:

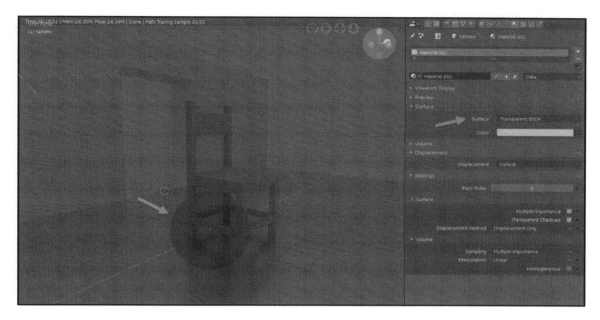

Figure 4.8: Transparent BSDF

That will give you pure transparency. If you want to smooth your sphere, you can press the Z key and choose **Shade Smooth** from the pie menu options.

For a more advanced transparency effect, you can choose the **Glass BSDF** shader. Set your material to use this shader and you will see an immediate change! Even the preview box from the material will display something close to a glass sphere, as shown in the following screenshot:

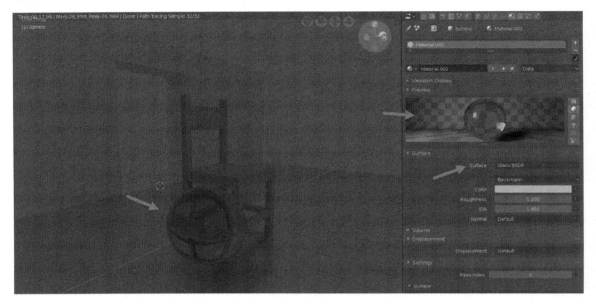

Figure 4.9: Glass material

You can control the level of light distortion caused by the glass with the IOR parameter.

Here are a few common values for IOR in transparent materials:

- Water: 1.3
- Glass: 1.5
- Plastic: 1.46
- Crystal: 2.0

You can easily find online lists with all kinds of transparent materials with IOR values.

Objects as light sources

What if you want to use an object as a light source? There is a shader that will help you achieve that type of effect. By selecting the **Emission** shader, you will be able to set an object as a light source. It will start to contribute to the scene lighting.

The shader is also simple and will offer you two options to control the color and strength of your light, as indicated in the next screenshot:

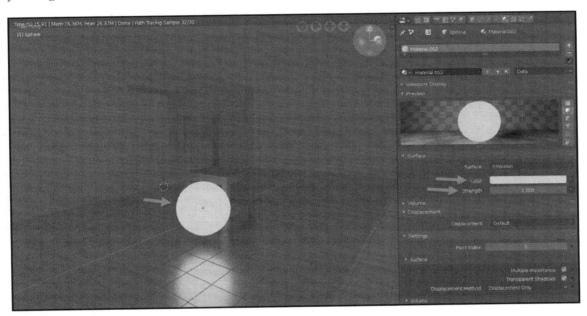

Figure 4.10: Objects as light sources

Multiple materials for one object

Having an object to display a single material is easy, but sometimes you might want to use multiple materials for the same object. For that purpose, you can use material indexes. Look at the top of your **Material** panel options, and you will see that each object has a list of indexes to work with. You will start with a single index, but you can add more with the + icon on the right and remove them using the - icon.

Unlike what many people think, when starting to use this feature, each index has a relation to an object and not a material. Note the following screenshot:

Figure 4.11: Material indexes

You can add new indexes to an object and assign preexisting materials to an object or create a new one.

At the right of your index selector, you will see plus and minus signs, which will give you control to either add or remove an index. But, to see all the controls, you must go to edit mode.

Once you select an object and enter edit mode, you will see **Assign**, **Select**, and **Deselect** options at the bottom, as shown in the following screenshot:

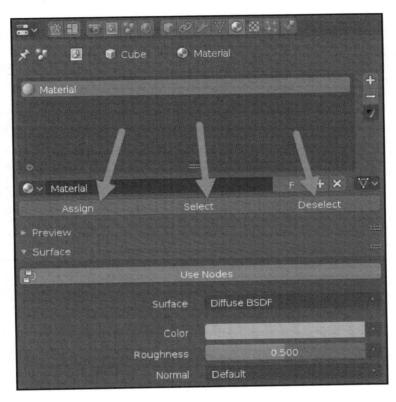

Figure 4.12: Index controls

For instance, select the chair model and, in edit mode, select only the top seat faces. Click the plus sign to create a new index, and add a new material by clicking on the **New** button. Set the material color to have a different tone from the overall chair.

In edit mode, click on the **Assign** button, and you will get that material applied to the face, as indicated in the next screenshot:

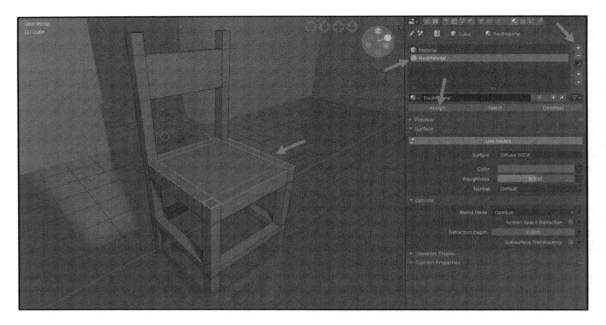

Figure 4.13: Multiple materials

You can use the same process to apply one material to each face of your object.

Summary

Materials are a great way to improve the realism of your scene, but they still lack in detail when compared to textures. In this chapter, learned the basics of managing and adding materials to Blender. In the next chapter, we will expand that knowledge. You will create materials that have textures to create something called PBR materials.

Real-Time Textures for Eevee 5

Using materials for objects in Blender is a great way to increase the realism for any project, but for most projects, a pure color won't be enough to produce excellent results. You will need textures!

In this chapter, you will learn how to add textures based on multiple maps for PBR materials, and also use the Shader editor.

Here is a list of what you will learn:

- How to use the Shader editor
- How to add textures to objects
- How to choose mapping options for textures
- How to use PBR textures in Blender
- How to pack textures to files

Technical requirements

You will be required to have Blender 2.80 installed to follow this procedure. Even if you have a later version of Blender, the described example should work with no significant problems.

The code files of this chapter can be found on GitHub: https://github.com/PacktPublishing/Blender-Quick-Start-Guide.

Check out the following video to see the code in action:

bit.ly/2xJVNZ3.

Working with textures in Eevee

Using textures on top of materials is a powerful way to boost the realism in almost all projects in Blender, and to add them to a texture is incredibly easy. There are a few things you have to understand before adding any texture:

- Textures are a part of materials. You need an object and an associated material.
- Textures will present themselves with one or multiple maps (images).
- The setup for textures will work much better in the shader editor.

Why do we have to set up textures in the shader editor? Since they use a lot of information and options for a proper setup, especially when we move to PBR textures, using the shader editor will give you more freedom.

The title of this chapter states "textures for Eevee," but everything we will do here also works for Cycles. In Blender, you can use all settings and parameters for materials and textures for both renderers.

Shader editor for textures

How do we use the shader editor? The first thing you will want to do is create a new division in the Blender user interface for a new window. If you are using the default window arrangement, change the timeline at the bottom for a shader editor, as indicated in the following screenshot:

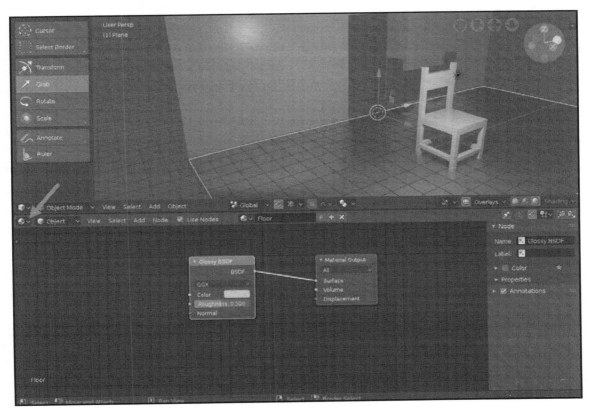

Figure 5.1: Shader editor window

When you open the shader editor, you will see something entirely new! In the preceding screenshot, you will see the material used for the floor in the model we've been working on since `Chapter 2`, *3D Modeling and Real-Time Render in Eevee.*

You can see two small boxes, which are nodes. There is a node for the **Glossy BSDF** and another called **Material Output**.

For materials, the only obligatory node is the **Material Output**, which is the node responsible for collecting all information and sending it to the object. Before that node, you can create multiple combinations with nodes to craft unique materials.

One thing you will notice about nodes is a number of small circles on the left or right of each box. Those are sockets and, depending on the node type, they might have input and output sockets, or just one type. For instance, you will see only input sockets for the **Material Output**, as indicated in the next screenshot:

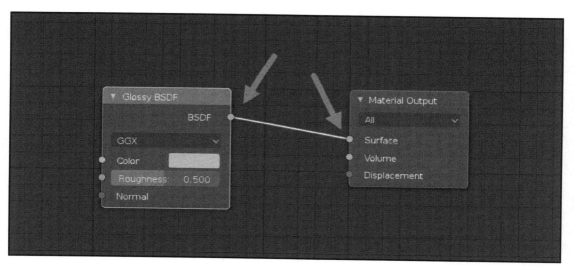

Figure 5.2: Sockets for nodes

As for the **Glossy BSDF**, you will see them both. Each socket will also show a color code representing the type of data they either accept, for input, or generate, for output. For instance, all shaders will have a green color code and output nodes have a red color code.

How do we connect nodes? All you have to do to connect them is click and drag from an output socket to an input. In the preceding screenshot, notice how the green output from **Glossy BSDF** has a connection to the green input of **Material Output**.

To break a connection, you can hold the *Ctrl* key and click and drag with the left mouse button. Your cursor will turn into a knife icon, and it will cut the lines.

Using image textures

To use image textures in Blender, you will first need a texture! From this point forward we will use a wood floor texture that you can download as part of the resources for the book. The texture has a Creative Commons 0 license, meaning it is in the public domain.

Look for the file called `WoodFloorColor.jpg` in `Chapter 5`, *Real-Time Textures for Eevee* resources. It is an image representing a wood floor showing only color information, as follows:

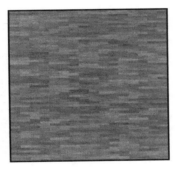

Figure 5.3: Color texture

You can use almost any type of image as a texture, but for the best results, you should look for the following:

- Square images and using a power of two as the size (512, 1024, 2048…)
- Seamless textures for better tiling options
- Textures in PBR format (more on that later in the chapter)

To use that image as a texture, we can use the **Glossy BSDF** and connect an image texture node to the input socket of its color property—the yellow circle on the left

Blender supports various formats of textures, but you should look for images in a PNG format for maximum quality. Those images usually use a compression that doesn't exclude data to reduce size.

In the shader editor, press the *Shift + A* keys or, using the **Add** menu, go to the texture group and choose **Image Texture**.

Click on the **Open** button and locate the texture file in your hard drive. After opening the texture file, click and drag from the color output of the texture to the color input of the **Glossy BSDF**—both of the yellow circles. Note the following screenshot:

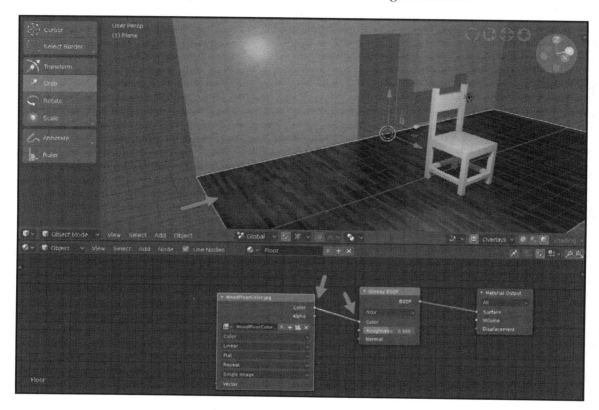

Figure 5.4: Wood floor texture

If you are using the 3D View shading in render mode, you will see the texture on the floor.

You can also drag and drop an image file from your file manager straight to Blender. If you release the file at the shader editor, Blender will automatically set it as an **Image texture** node.

To control the size and repetition of such a texture, we will also need a mapping node. If you look at the Image Texture node, it has only one purple input called Vector.

Using the *Shift + A* or **Add** menu, go to the **Vector** group and choose **Mapping**, as indicated in the next screenshot:

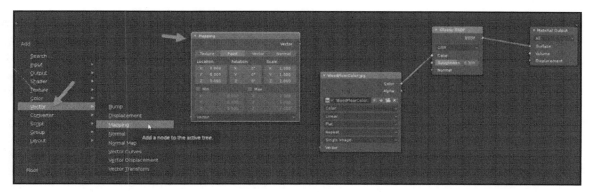

Figure 5.5: Controlling mapping

Once you connect the mapping output to the Image Texture, you will notice that your texture will look weird in the plane. That is because we also need a texture coordinate node. Press, once again, *Shift + A*, or the **Add** menu, and in the **Input** group add a **Texture Coordinate** node, as indicated in the following screenshot:

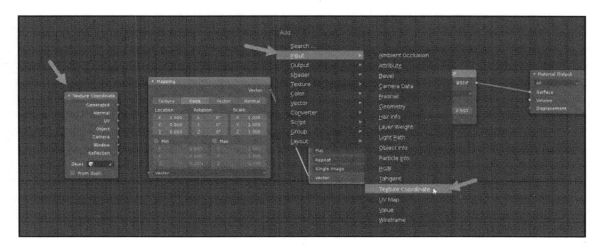

Figure 5.6 - Texture coordinate

Connect the generated output of the **Texture Coordinate** to the input of your **Mapping,** and you will have the texture back at the plane.

You will get a basic template for all other image textures you might want to use in the future. If you replace the image texture file and shader, for something like a **Diffuse BSDF,** you can get any color texture in your scene.

To control the tiling of your image, you can use the scale options in the **Mapping** node, as indicated in the next screenshot:

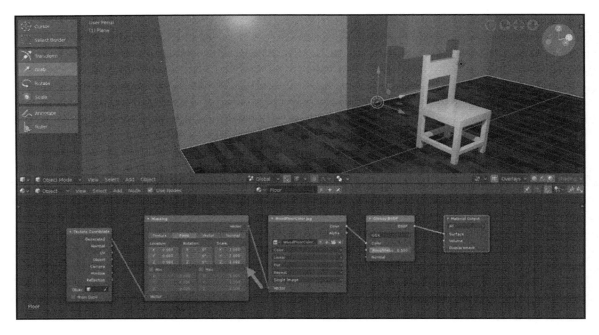

Figure 5.7: Scale option

They will work almost like a repetition control. For instance, if you set the scale for both **X** and **Y** as 2, you will get the texture repeated twice in the same space on both axes.

Using a PBR material

Since Chapter 4, *Using Real-Time Materials in Eevee*, we have been talking about PBR materials, and it is finally time to start using them in Blender. But what are PBR materials? The acronym **PBR** stands for **Physically Based Rendering**. That means a PBR material will have a lot of the physical properties of a real-world surface.

To achieve that surface, it needs much more than a simple image texture file. You will need several files to represent each aspect of a surface.

Nowadays, it is relatively simple to find PBR materials online on both paid and free material libraries. To show you how to create a PBR material, we will use a version of the same wood floor material from the beginning of this chapter.

You can download a file called WoodFloorPBR.zip to your hard drive.

Inside the ZIP, you will find four maps with images for the following:

- Color
- Ambient Occlusion
- Normal
- Roughness

Those maps will help you create a realistic material.

The first step to add a PBR material to the floor of our scene is to remove the existing material from the object. Use the **X** button to remove the material and create a new material, as shown in the following screenshot:

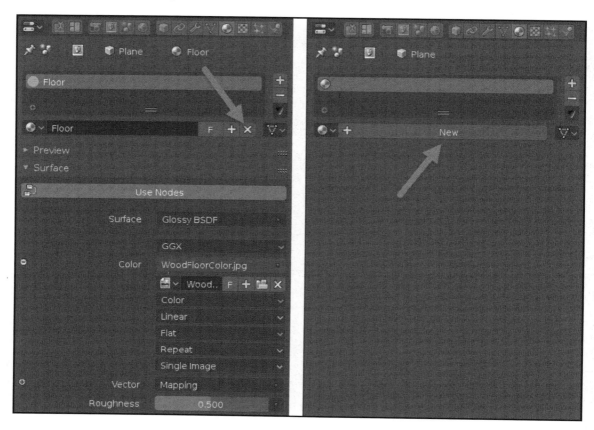

Figure 5.8: Creating a new material

In your newly created material, you will get the **Principled BSDF** shader, and that is the proper option for PBR materials.

Add a **Texture Coordinate** and **Mapping** nodes using the same options from the previous section of this chapter. Connect the first two, and we will have a basic template for the PBR material, shown as follows:

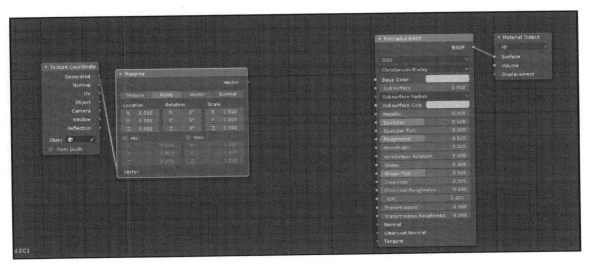

Figure 5.9: PBR template

Adding multiple image textures

Our PBR texture has a total of four different maps we can use, and because of that, you will also need four Image Texture nodes. Add one to the material using either the *Shift + A* keys or the **Add** menu. Select the node with a right-click; you can duplicate the node three times. Note the following screenshot:

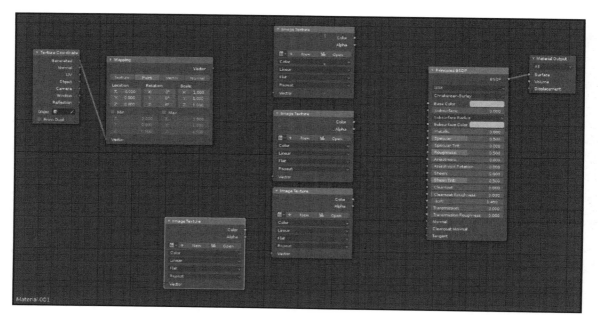

Figure 5.10: Multiple image nodes

You can use almost all shortcut keys from the 3D View in the shader editor.

The next step is to open each one of the maps for the image texture nodes. If you want to follow an order you can do so as follows:

- Color
- Ambient occlusion
- Normal
- Roughness

Mixing nodes with color and ambient occlusion

Usually, you will connect each image texture to a corresponding input socket in a node. For instance, you will find that we have a roughness input socket and a texture called roughness. But we don't have anything that looks like ambient occlusion. How do we connect the texture?

In this case, we have to blend the ambient occlusion with the color texture.

Using the *Shift + A* keys or the **Add** menu, go to the **Color** group and pick a **MixRGB** node. Change the node mode to **Multiply** and connect the output of both image textures' color and ambient occlusion maps.

And finally, you can connect the output from the **MixRGB** to the **Base Color** of your **Principled BSDF**:

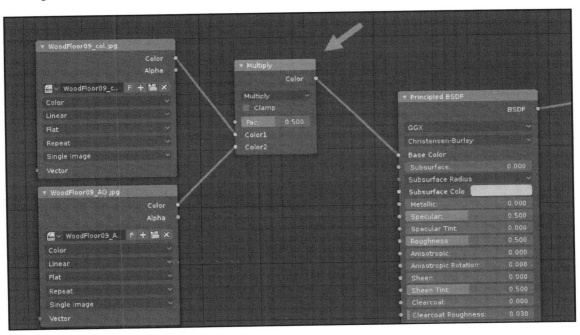

Figure 5.11: Mixing two image textures

Using a normal map

A normal map will give you a layer of detail for materials in 3D with no need to add new geometry to a 3D model. Using such a map will make small elevations on a surface based on a map.

If you look at our normal map texture, shown in the following image, you will see a strange arrangement of colors:

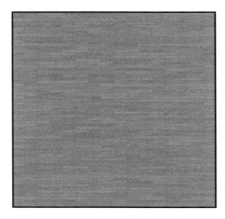

Figure 5.12: Normal map

Using the information from the texture, Blender will try to create the wood plank shapes on the object surface. It won't be the same as making them using polygons, but it will be enough to give a sensation that something is there representing the wood.

The **Principled BSDF** node has a normal input, but it won't accept the image texture directly. We need an intermediate node. You will have to press the *Shift + A* keys or the **Add** menu to create from the **Vector** group a **Normal Map** node.

Then, you can connect the normal texture to the **Normal Map** node, and finally get it to the **Principled BSDF**. Unlike the color and ambient occlusion, we won't use the color data from our image texture. Change the data type of your image texture to **Non-Color Data**, as indicated in the next screenshot:

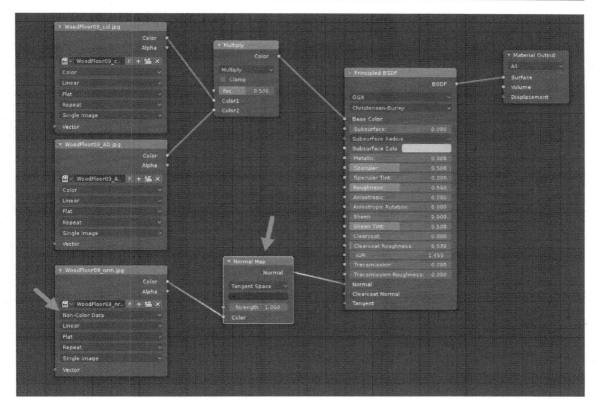

Figure 5.13: Normal map node

You can control the intensity of your normal texture using the **Strength** value in the **Normal Map** node.

Adding a roughness texture

The most comfortable image texture to add for our PBR material is the roughness, which you can connect directly to the **Principled BSDF**. For this, we won't use any color data, which will require you to also change the type at the top of your node.

Finishing up the PBR material

As for the last step for your PBR material, we can connect the output of our **Mapping** node to all four image texture inputs. It might look confusing at first, but it follows a flow of information from left to right that gives artists a powerful tool for crafting materials.

Summary

With the basis to create PBR materials and add textures to objects in Blender, we can move to better rendering and light controls. You will see that all textures will eventually look much better in scenes that also have a realistic light.

In the next chapter, you will learn how to use environment lights and better controls over rendering with Eevee.

6
Lights and Real-Time Rendering with Blender Eevee

One of the critical subjects that most artists want to improve in their projects is lighting. In Blender, you have some options that allow you to create a beautiful light setup with just a few clicks, with the use of environmental textures for both Eevee and Cycles.

That is the main subject of this chapter, which will describe ways to improve and get much better lighting for your scenes.

In this chapter you will learn how to:

- Use environment lights to improve your scenes
- Control aspects of lighting, such as exposure and contrast
- Apply color correction
- Use post-processing effects for your scene

Technical requirements

You will be required to have Blender 2.80 installed to follow this procedure. Even if you have a later version of Blender, the described example should work with no significant problems.

The code files of this chapter can be found on GitHub:
`https://github.com/PacktPublishing/Blender-Quick-Start-Guide`.

Check out the following video to see the code in action:

`bit.ly/2QhS63L`.

Rendering with Blender Eevee

How can we improve the lighting for any scene in Blender? A powerful yet simple way to achieve much better results for lighting is to use an environment texture. This is a texture that you will place in the background of your scene that will contribute to the lighting of your scene, and also provide something to be reflected off of glossy surfaces.

The place to add such textures in Blender is the World tab in your properties window. There you will find a field called **Surface**, as shown here:

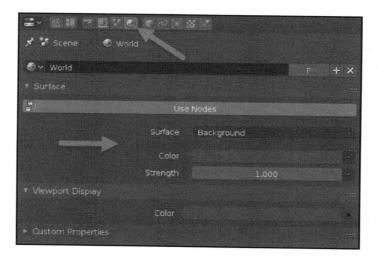

 If you can't see all surface options, it is probably because you must also turn on the **Use Nodes** button.

To get a texture to work as an environment map, you will need a particular type of image, called **high dynamic range** (HDR). An HDR image is something like a 360° photo that will surround your scene from all sides, and can also contribute to the lighting of your project.

Using an HDR texture as background

Unlike regular textures that you must assign to materials in Blender, you will add the HDR texture to the color section of your world. Notice that you have a color selector that will let you set a color for the background. On the right side of that selector, you will see a small button with a circle in the middle.

Click on that button and choose **Environment Texture** from the options.

You will see something strange happening to your scene—it will turn completely pink. Blender uses this color to visually display an error when it can't find a particular texture.

Click on the **Open** button from the new options that will appear in the world settings and pick the HDR file. You will see the image as your background, which should look something like this:

You can download this image file, called `park.hdr`, from the resources of this chapter. Using the **Strength** option, you can control how intense the light that comes from your HDR map will be.

Assuming you have your 3D View shading set to render, the scene will immediately start to render an improved version of your scene lights.

Adding shadows with Eevee

One aspect of your lights with environment maps that you will miss with Eevee is the lack of shadows. At the moment, Eevee won't display shadows from such light sources. If you want to improve the scene with shadows, you can use a lamp in your scene.

A sun lamp will do the trick, and you can use the existing lamp and turn that into a sun. If you select the light and open the Data panel in your properties window, you will be able to swap between all lamp types, as shown here:

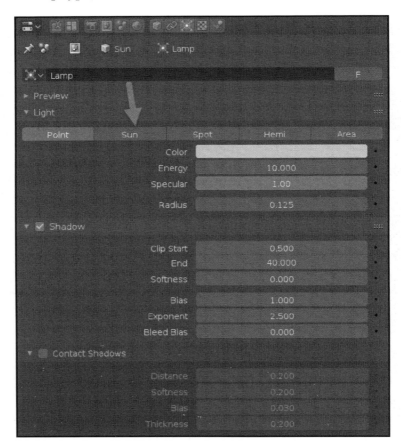

Click on the **Sun** button and your lamp will become a sun! One of the main advantages of using a sun is that you will have shadows in the scene, and also be able to adjust the way the shadows behave visually.

At the top, you have options to set the color and intensity (strength) of your light. A critical setting that you will want to adjust is **Softness** (see the following screenshot). Using that parameter will give you control over the shape of your lights. Lower values will give hard-edged shadows, while raising the values will result in a blurred border for shadows:

You can select the lamp and use the *R* key to control the direction of your light.

Effects and options for Eevee

Besides having the benefit of showing real-time materials and lights in your 3D View, Eevee will also offer a variety of options for effects. One of these effects is already in use for our materials; that is, the **Screen Space Reflections** effect, as shown in the following screenshot:

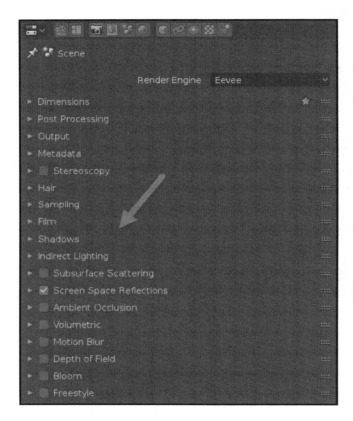

These effects will help you create a more compelling image in real time, and will also boost realism in many cases. For instance, you can turn on **Ambient Occlusion** to generate contact shadows for objects.

All effects in the following list will only work for Blender Eevee.

Bloom effect

A bloom effect is common in the real-time engines used in games, and you can take advantage of such an effect in Blender as well. When you turn on this effect, you will see a glowing light from all surfaces receiving direct lights.

You can enable the effect with the small checkbox on the left of the bloom effect option, as shown in the following screenshot:

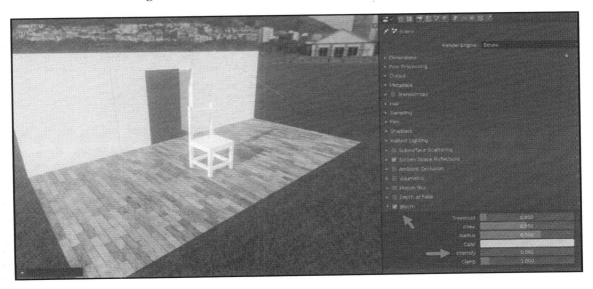

Using the intensity value, you can control the strength of your bloom.

Shadow quality

Shadow quality is not an effect, but it could help you with the visual results of a render. Have you noticed how shadows are somehow low quality in your renders? In Eevee, you will get real-time shadows based on a projection size that you can control in the **Shadows** field, as shown here:

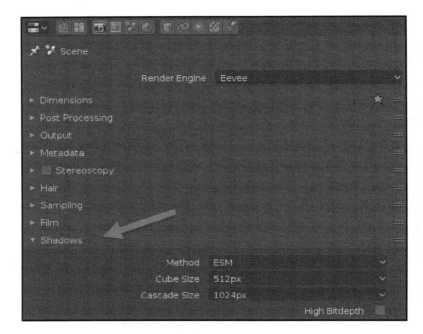

Look at the **Cascade Size** parameter. This is set to **1024px** by default. If you increase this to **4096px**, you will see a much better shadow projection, as shown here:

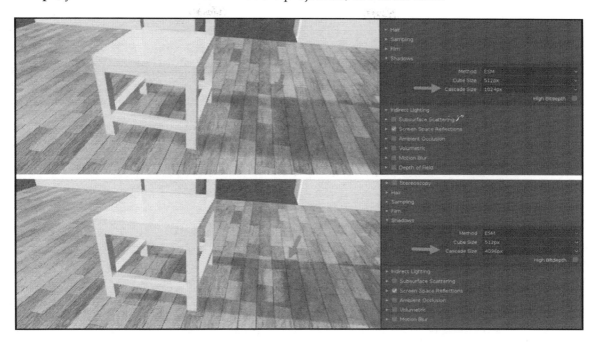

Despite being a great option to improve your shadows, using such a choice might add a significant computational load to the project.

Sampling

The default quality for rendering in Eevee will be enough for most projects, but you can increase the final result using the sampling panel shown here:

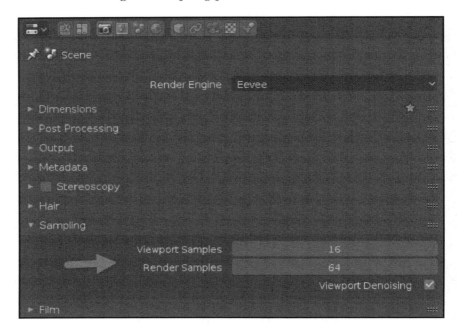

There, you will find two options:

- Viewport samples
- Render samples

With the first option, you can set the quality, or level of noise, for images in your 3D View. For final results and saving renders as images, you can increase values for the second option. If you want better images with less noise, a value of 128 for the render samples will give excellent results.

Removing the background for rendering

If you want to render an image that doesn't show your HDR map as the background, you can set that in your **Film** settings. Here, you will see the **Alpha** setting, with two simple options to choose from.

You can pick **Sky** to give you a full background image for renders, or choose **Transparent** to completely remove your HDR map (or anything else) as shown in the following screenshot:

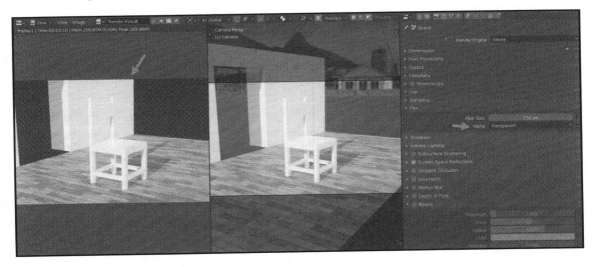

To save an image with a transparent background, you should pick the PNG format with RGBA color.

Using a light probe to boost indirect lighting

A light probe is a new type of object, introduced in Blender 2.8, to help Eevee achieve excellent results with indirect light. It works by creating a volume in which the software can calculate indirect light bounces inside that area.

Besides indirect light bounces, you will also get better reflections for glossy materials.

For instance, you can create a light probe, called an irradiance volume, using the *Shift + A* keys or the **Add** menu. Go to the **Light Probe** group and choose **Irradiance Volume**, as shown here:

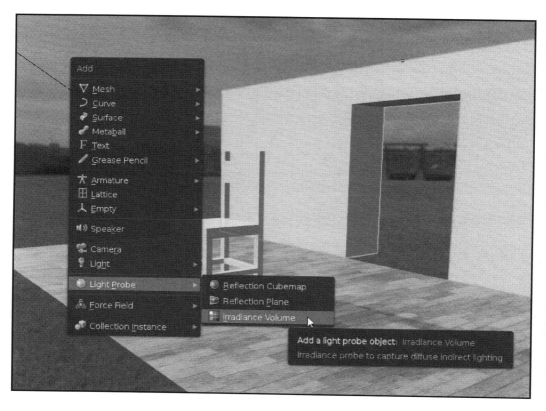

When you first create the object, the irradiance volume will be a small box . Use the *S* key to scale the box, and adjust it so that your scene fits inside. You can also scale the object on one axis only to better fit the scene if needs be, as shown here:

Using an **Irradiance Volume** for external scenes won't make much of a difference. The effect will appear more strongly in interior scenes where indirect lights will play a more significant role in lighting.

The **Irradiance Volume** will process all information related to lights inside its area. As a result, you will get an improved indirect light effect.

Rendering with Cycles

Using **Eevee** will give you the joy of seeing all the effects and lights in real time, but sometimes you might need higher quality for your images. In this case, you should use **Cycles** as your renderer. The good news is that almost all settings from **Eevee** are compatible with Cycles, so you won't have to change materials or world settings.

All you have to do is change the main renderer from **Eevee** to **Cycles** , as shown here:

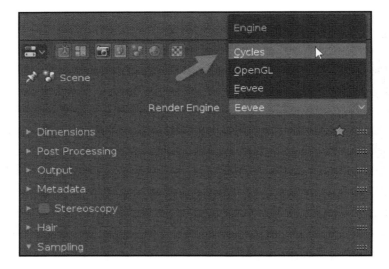

If you have the shading of your 3D View set to rendered, you will start to see an immediate change to how Blender will process the scene. First, your scene will appear with a lot of noise, and a counter will appear at the top of your 3D View. Once it reaches 32 (the default value), it will stop processing the scene.

In the end, you will have a grainy version of the render that might look something like this:

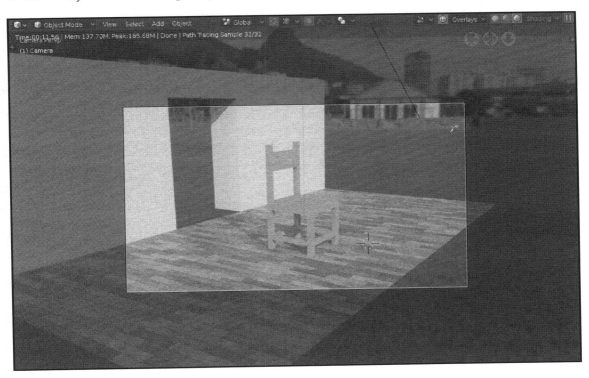

Cycles uses something called progressive refinement to get a final image, and in theory, you could let it keep processing the image forever. Since you would probably not like to wait that long, it uses a limit to stop calculations. That is the sample count.

You can set the limits using the sampling options in your render panel, as shown here:

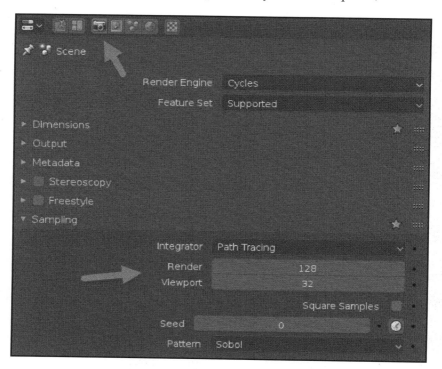

By default, Blender will use a sample count of **32** for a preview in the 3D View, and **128** for renders. What would be a good value for renders? That will depend on your scene. Here is an example of our scene rendered with a limit of 500 samples:

A **side effect** of having a high value as the limit is that you will have to wait a little longer to render. For instance, our preview with 32 samples took about 15 seconds to render. A render with 500 samples required 240 seconds.

Other variables will also influence how long a render will take. For instance, the resolution you choose to render an image at is a crucial point.

Enabling your GPU for rendering

If you have a modern GPU in your computer or laptop, you can use it to significantly increase the speed at which Cycles processes a scene. Nowadays, you can use both hardware from Nvidia or AMD to get faster results, and Cycles will send all processing to those devices.

To use a GPU, you will first have to make sure that Blender recognizes your device. Go to the **Edit** menu and choose **User Preferences**. There, choose the **System** tab and look for the **Cycles Compute Device** options, as shown in the following screenshot:

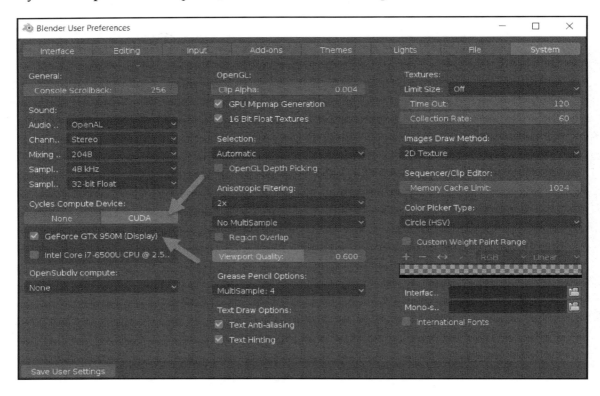

After you check that Cycles can use your device, you must also set the performance settings to **GPU Compute**, as shown here:

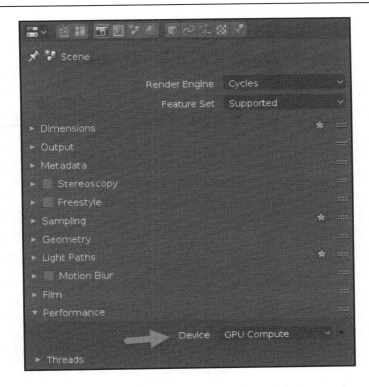

How fast can you render with a GPU? Just for comparison, I did a render of the same scene using both CPU and GPU. With a resolution of 960 x 540 pixels and 500 samples:

- **CPU**: 195 seconds to render
- **GPU**: 133 seconds to render

A reduction in render times of about 32%! The performance gains will depend on the hardware you have—high-end GPUs will give you an incredible speed boost in Cycles.

Removing the background and noise

If you also want to remove the background from your render in Cycles, in the render options you will find a similar panel to that in Eevee. There, you can turn on **Transparency** in the **Film** settings, as shown here:

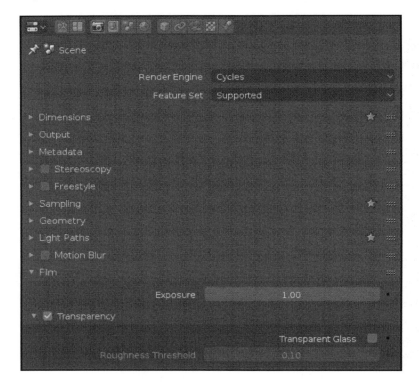

And your render will have a transparent background. Just remember to save your files as a PNG, with the RGBA option checked, to keep that transparency in the final image.

To apply a filter to your render and reduce the amount of noise, you can turn on the **Denoising** option in your **Viewport** tab in the properties window, shown in the following screenshot. Using the default settings of the filter will already give you a significant reduction in noise:

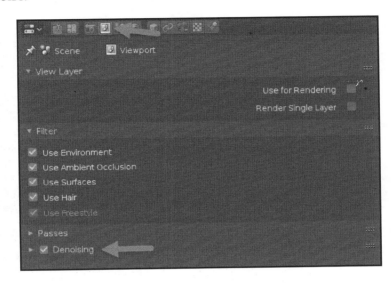

The filter will apply a small amount of blur to your images and provide noise reduction for your projects.

Color and exposure controls

If you think the scene you are working at the moment still needs additional lights, you can try to increase the exposure of your scene. Just like in photography, the exposure will let more light into the camera, resulting in a brighter image.

Blender has exposure controls for both **Cycles** and **Eevee** at the same location. You will find these in the **Scene** tab in your properties window.

Look for the **Color Management** options, and you will find the exposure settings as follows:

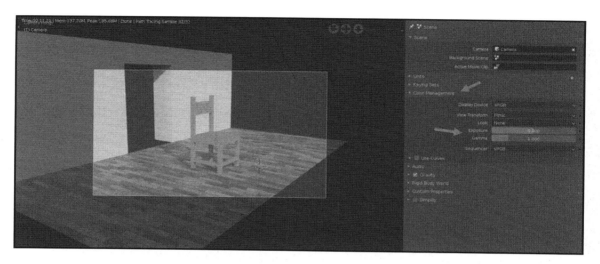

With a default value of zero, you will get a standard exposure for all scenes, but raising it to something like 1.5 will make any scene brighter, as shown in this screenshot:

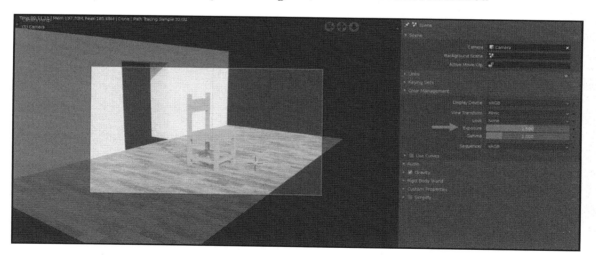

Summary

Light and rendering are complex subjects with a lot of small options that could set the direction of your project. You could either get a realistic image, or something that looks like an obvious computer graphics image. Now you know how to configure a scene and render with both Eevee and Cycles.

The next chapter will introduce you to animation, and we will create a small intro for a video using 3D text and some camera settings.

7
Animate Everything in Blender 2.8!

Blender is a great tool for creating realistic images of interiors and products, but you will also find a lot of options to make videos and animations. From a simple motion graphics intro for a video to character animation, you can quickly make your ideas come alive with Blender.

In this chapter, we will explore the possibilities of video animation with Blender by creating a quick intro for a video. You will learn how to do the following:

- Set up an orthographic camera for video
- Add keyframes for interpolation-based animation
- Create 3D text for video
- Insert keyframes for any properties in Blender

By the end of this chapter, you will have an intro video, that you can use for any production, and that will display the title of your project.

Technical requirements

You will need to have Blender 2.80 installed to follow this procedure. Even if you have a later version of Blender, the described example should work with no significant problems.

The code files of this chapter can be found on GitHub:
`https://github.com/PacktPublishing/Blender-Quick-Start-Guide`.

Check out the following video to see the code in action:

`bit.ly/2OXBhuw.`

How animation works in Blender 2.8

A key feature for most 3D tools, such as Blender, is the ability to create animations from 3D objects that you can render into a video. The video could go in all types of production, from feature films to your YouTube channel.

The easiest way to create animations in Blender is with the use of keyframes and interpolation. You can add keyframes to objects in the 3D View and all other windows in Blender. In the user interface, you will see that most properties in Blender can be animated.

Some properties that we will animate won't display a preview in 3D View, but you will be able to see the changes once we get the animation as a video.

Creating the scene for our animation

Before we start to dive into animation and how you can move things around in Blender, we must create a basic scene first. The project we will develop is a quick intro scene for a video. It could be the titles or intro scene for your YouTube channel.

The scene will be relatively simple and will feature a text video with titles and your channel name at the bottom, as shown here:

Our animation plans are simple and involve getting both text objects entering the screen from the left and right sides. The main title will slide in from the left and the channel name from the right. In the following, you can see the layout for our animation:

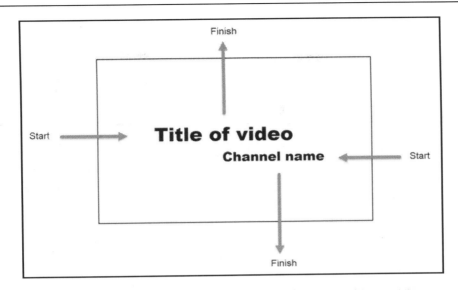

Since both of our objects are text, we must begin with their creation. How do we create text in Blender? Using the *Shift + A* keys or the **Add** menu, you will see an option with the name **Text**, as shown here:

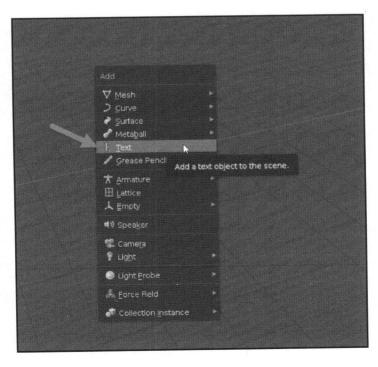

Once you add the text to the scene, you will probably want to change the default text from **Text** to something else. You can get access to the contents of a text object by selecting it and entering Edit mode.

In **Edit Mode**, you can change your text just like in any regular text editor. Using the backspace or *Del* keys, you can erase the default content and type your new text. In the following, I have typed the text `Blender Review`:

Go back to **Object Mode** and, using the *Shift + D* keys, we can duplicate the title and move it to the bottom. For the second line, you can change the text from 3D Artist to your channel name. Use the *S* key to shrink down your text a little:

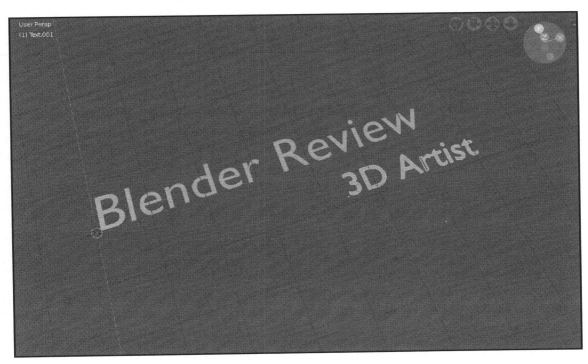

In the preceding screenshot, you can see two important text options highlighted. In the **Object Data** tab in the properties window, you will see options for any selected 3D text in Blender.

You can set an extrude for the text in the top options of the tab, and also change the text font. To change your font, you have to load your chosen font file in Blender. Use the folder icon to locate the font file in your operation system, as shown here:

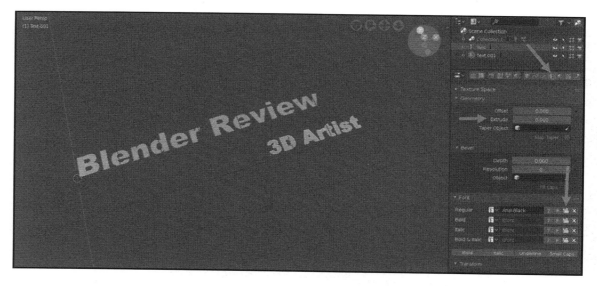

You can choose different fonts for regular, bold, and italic text.

Making an orthographic camera for video

The camera for a text-based animation will be slightly different from what we had in our 3D scenes. An orthographic view of the project will be the best choice to mimic a flat 2D space.

You can change the Blender camera to orthographic mode easily in the properties. First, we must place it looking from top to bottom. Using the 7 key on the numpad, or the Z icon in your widget navigator (the blue circle with a Z inside), set the 3D View to the top.

Use the *Ctrl + Alt+ 0* (on the numpad) keys to align your camera with your actual view. Or you can also go to the **View** menu, then **Align View**, then lastly **Align Active Camera to View**.

Now, select the camera border, and in the properties window for that object, you will see an option called **Type** at the top. Change that to **Orthographic**, as shown here:

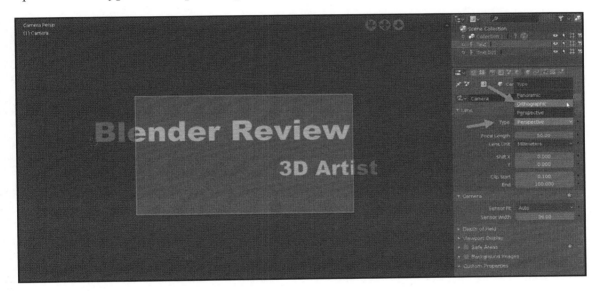

As a last step for the camera, we have to frame the text in the center. Using the *G* key will be enough to move your camera to the sides, and with the orthographic scale you can choose the camera's proximity to the text, as shown in the following screenshot. At the bottom, you can also turn on composition guides to display guidelines in the camera. Turn on **Center** and **Golden**, as follows:

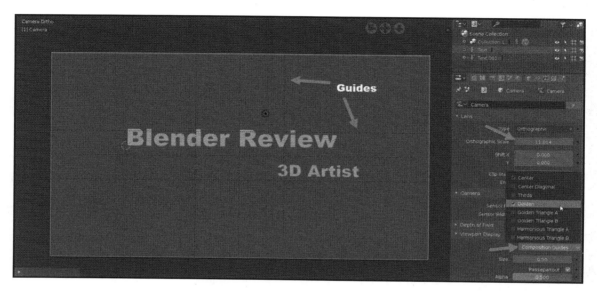

Animation with keyframes in Blender

Blender works with something called interpolation-based animation, which will allow you to create automated animations based on the differences between two properties on a timeline.

To make the process easier to understand, have a look at this diagram:

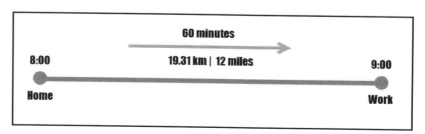

Imagine a simple scenario where you have to go from home to work between 8:00 and 9:00 in the morning. You have the timeline and a difference in locations for a subject (in this case, you). Therefore, for the animation, we have the following properties:

- Time
- Distance and location

With regard to time in animations, you will find that Blender uses frames instead of seconds, minutes, or hours. For each second you will get 24 frames, which you can change later.

 24 frames per second is an industry standard, but you can use whatever speed you need. You can change this in the Render panel, under Frame Rate settings.

If we replace some of the information from the preceding diagram with a 3D object that must move from one location to another, we will have something like the following:

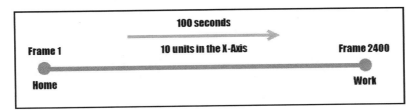

As for timing, we have our motion happening between **Frame 1** and **2,400**. That will work out to **100** seconds of motion. Our object must move from coordinates 0,0,0 to 10,0,0. As a result, the object will move in a straight line along the **X-axis**.

Since this is an interpolation-based animation, you will have the software doing the math for you and calculating all the positions needed for motion. To get from 0 to 10 in a total of 12 frames, your object must advance 0.004 units on each frame.

Inserting keyframes for animation

Using a window, such as the timeline, to manipulate animation time easily is a significant help for projects such as the one we are trying to create. Assuming you are using the default interface for Blender, a timeline window will be available at the bottom of your screen.

If not, you can create a division on the interface and change the window type to Timeline. The timeline is highlighted:

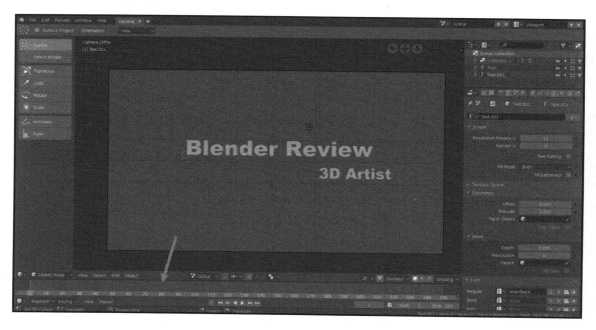

Before we proceed, make sure you have the text aligned to the center of your camera frame. Having the object in the final stage of animation is not a problem for Blender, and sometimes it is easier to start backward.

We can set the keyframes to mark all the positions where the objects will be at the end of the animation. Later, we will set how they will look at the beginning.

The animation will have text coming from both sides for 1 second (24 frames), and will have them stay still for 8 seconds (192 frames). After that time, both text components will exit the screen to the top and bottom in 1 second (24 frames). There will be a total of 24+192+24 = 240 frames.

Set the end animation parameter of our project to 240 in the timeline window, and move the playback head (the vertical blue line) until it reaches frame 24, as follows:

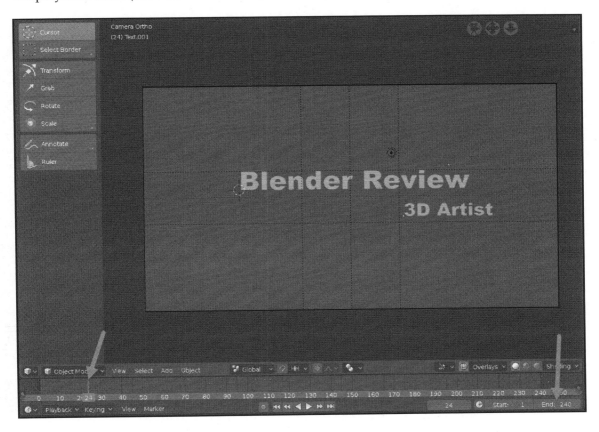

Select both text objects and press the *I* key. Blender will display a list of keyframe types that you can insert into objects, as shown here:

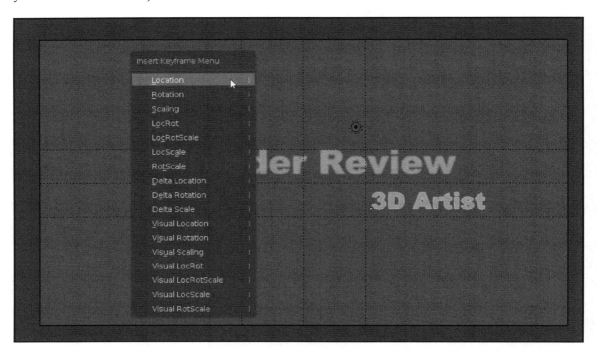

Our animation will use location-based movement, which requires a Location keyframe. Pick this option. In the Timeline window, you will see an orange diamond when you select an object that has keyframes.

 If you plan to use other types of animation, you must pick an equivalent keyframe type. For instance, an animation dealing with object size would need a Scaling keyframe.

Move the playback head to frame 216 and add another keyframe to both text objects, using the Location option.

With keyframes at position 24 (1 second) and 216 (8 seconds), we won't have any movement from both objects. They will stay still.

Set the playback head to frame 1, and move the top text object outside your camera frame, to the left of it. Do the same with the lower object, but to the right-hand side. Add one location keyframe for each object at frame 1, as follows:

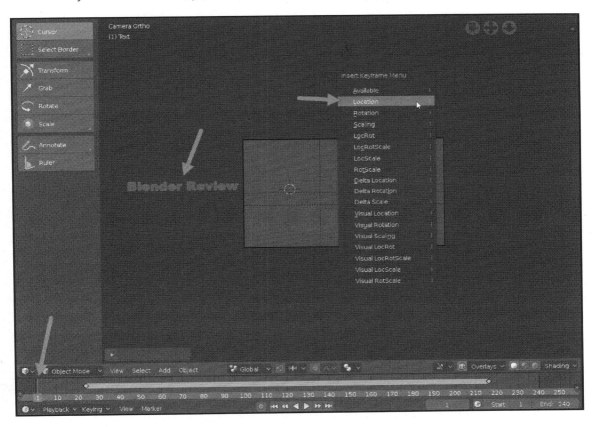

You will see keyframes set for both text objects in frame 1. Do you want to see a preview of the animation? You can click on the Play button in the Timeline window, or use the *Shift +* Spacebar keys.

Finally, move the playback head to frame 240. Both objects will go back to the center of your screen once you set the frame to 240. Select the top text and move it outside your camera frame, but toward the top. Do the same for the lower text, but move it to the bottom.

With the two objects selected, press the *I* key and choose **Location**, as shown in the following screenshot. We now have all keyframes set for motion!

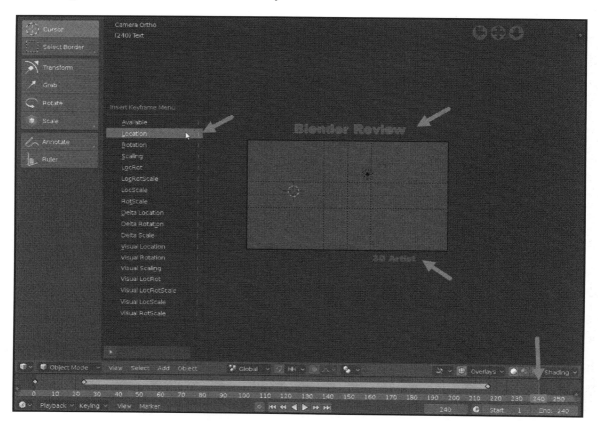

Since Blender uses interpolation to create movement, it will calculate all positions between keyframes automatically.

Press Play to see a preview of our animation.

 You can use the *Shift* + left arrow keys on your keyboard to quickly set the playback head to the first frame of your timeline.

Animation using properties

Besides adding keyframes to objects using the *I* key in Blender in 3D View, you can also animate almost any property in the software. The process is simple and requires you to follow the same procedure we've just used to get something moving around.

You can add keyframes to anything in Blender that has a small black dot on the right side of a given property, as shown here:

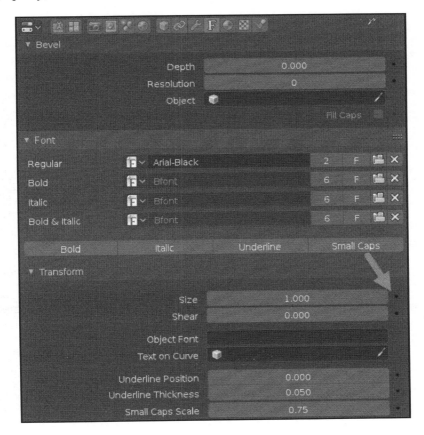

When you click on that black dot, you will add a keyframe to the value. Another way to add a keyframe is by placing the mouse cursor on top of the property and pressing the *I* key.

We can add an animation to the text font using the **Size** property. The animation will happen between frames 24 and 216.

Set your playback head to frame 24 and select the text representing the title of your video. Press the small black dot to the right of the **Size** property. The background of your property will assume a yellow color, as shown here:

Repeat the same process for the lower text.

Move the playback head to frame 216, change the size property for both text objects to 1.1, and add another keyframe for each of them.

That will create a subtle animation, with the text objects slightly growing in size from frame 24 to 216.

Always change the playback head before you change any property for animation. If you change the property value first, Blender will try to set the value for your current frame.

If you can't see the preview animation using the *Shift* + Spacebar keys, you can set the current frame to 24 and press *F12* to see a still render. Repeat the process with frame 216, and you will see a preview for the end part of your animation. For a property that has an animation, you will see a green background color between values receiving that are being interpolated.

Summary

You now have an excellent basis on which to make animations in Blender using keyframes and interpolation-based movement! In the next chapter, we will improve the animation by adding a moving background, and find out how you can edit and render the full video.

8
Editing Animations in Blender 2.8

Whenever you have a project related to animation in Blender, you will probably want to make adjustments to its timing and speed. For this type of adjustment in animations, you will have to manipulate keyframes, moving them in your timeline.

This chapter will explain how you can make changes to timing and enhancements to animations, including the following:

- Editing movement timing
- Changing keyframe position
- Creating animation loops
- Using the video sequencer to add sound
- Rendering animations as video

Technical requirements

You will need to have Blender 2.80 installed to follow this procedure. Even if you have a later version of Blender, the described example should work with no significant problems.

The code files of this chapter can be found on GitHub:
`https://github.com/PacktPublishing/Blender-Quick-Start-Guide`.

Check out the following video to see the code in action:

`bit.ly/2QeaJ8m`.

How to edit animations in Blender 2.8

Making an animation in Blender with keyframes is just the first step in the production of a video. After adding and setting all keyframes, you will probably want to change the timing. Something may be moving too quickly or slowly, and you will need to change such a behavior.

In Blender, you can change timing using the timeline window and the keyframe representation. Look at the window, and you will see that all keyframes appear as small diamond-shaped icons.

If you right-click on one of those icons, you will select a keyframe, as shown here:

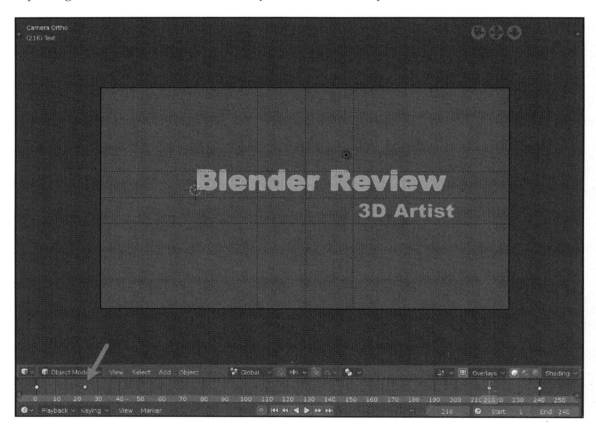

Editing and moving keyframes

Once you select a keyframe, it is easy to move and edit it. There are two options for moving keyframes:

- Click and drag with the right mouse button
- Use the *G* key to move objects around

In the timeline window, and all other parts of Blender, you can use the same shortcut keys to manage selections:

- *A* **key**: Select all keyframes
- *Alt + A* **keys**: Deselect all keyframes
- *B* **key**: Box-select keyframes
- *G* **key**: Move keyframes
- *S* **key**: Scale keyframe distance

For instance, we can make the entrance of your text a little faster by moving the keyframe from position 24 to 16. Moving two keyframes closer to each other means the animation will be faster.

You can also delete keyframes in the timeline by selecting them and pressing the *Del* or *X* keys.

Select the title text, and in the timeline select the second keyframe at position 24. Using the *G* key or by dragging your mouse, move it to position 16, as shown here:

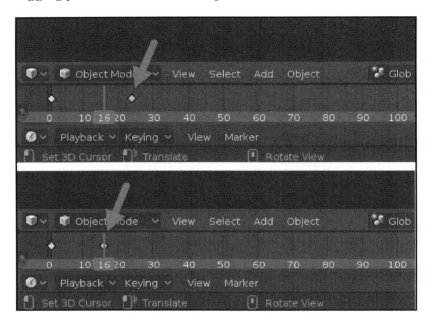

Repeat the same process with the lower text, and by hitting the Play button to preview your animation you will see the text enter your screen much more quickly. That is a natural process for most animation producers.

First, you will block the movement to get a rough workflow with all movements, and then later you can edit and set more accurate timings for all objects.

As a way to improve your project even further, you could also make the text exit the screen faster. Move all keyframes from position 216 to something like 230. This gives the objects just ten frames in which to exit your screen.

Creating an animated background for video

At this point, you can render any frame in your animation, and it will display your text with a gray background only. Wouldn't it be great to add a backdrop to the scene? It could be something like an animated background.

The plan when creating a background for our video is to add a plane at the bottom of our scene and insert a texture onto the object. Using a plane will allow us to create an animation for it later.

Using the *Shift + A* keys or the **Add** menu, create a plane and align it to the center of your scene. Make sure the plane stays behind both text objects, and if necessary, move it down along the Z-axis. Your final layout should look something like the following:

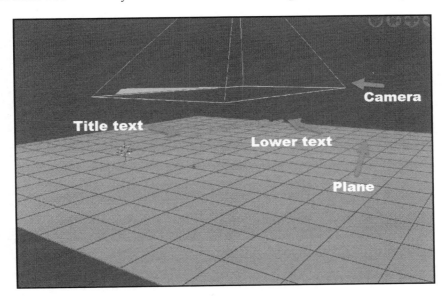

You can use the *S* key to adjust the scale of your plane.

Now, add a material to the plane. Using an image texture, you can set the background. You can download the texture for this plane from this book's resources.

You can easily swap windows in Blender to add and adjust materials. In the timeline window, use the selector to view the Shader Editor for your material. Once you finish editing the material, go back to the timeline.

In the plane texture settings, you only need to adjust the scale settings. In my case, using a scale of **8** for both the **X** and **Y** axes will result in a reasonable size for the texture, as shown here:

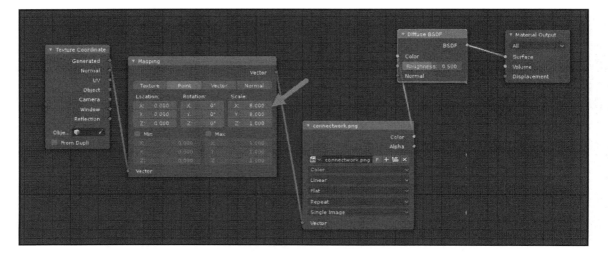

If you render the scene now, you should see the background with its texture, as follows:

TIP

To remove the shadows from your text, you can disable shadow casting in the lamp object's settings.

Creating loops for animation

A static background might work well for some projects, but since we have a full 3D tool such as Blender available, making an animated background will look way better.

The plan is to make our plane rotate along the Z-axis, making a 360° turn from frame 1 to 120, repeating the process on a loop. Using that technique will allow you to make an animated background compatible with almost any project length. No matter whether you have 240 or 240,000 frames, Blender will keep spinning your plane.

As a first step, we have to set the pivot point of your plane. What is the best location? Somewhere near the center of your camera framing. You can use the composite guides of your camera to place the 3D cursor near the center, as shown here:

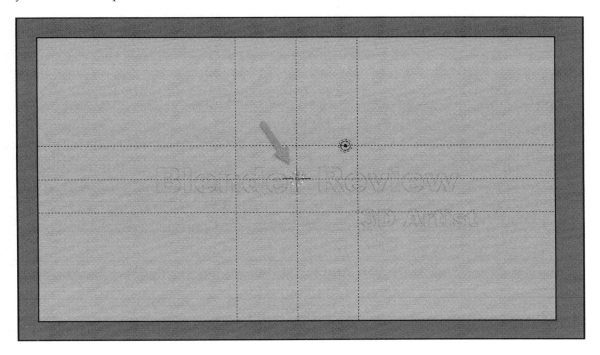

Use the left mouse button to place your 3D cursor, and with the plane selected, go to the **Object** menu and choose **Transformation**, then **Origin to 3D Cursor**. That will move your origin point to the cursor location.

It is time to add keyframes to our plane with a slightly different strategy from before. Set the playback head to 1 on your timeline, and add a keyframe to the plane, choosing Rotation as the type, as shown here:

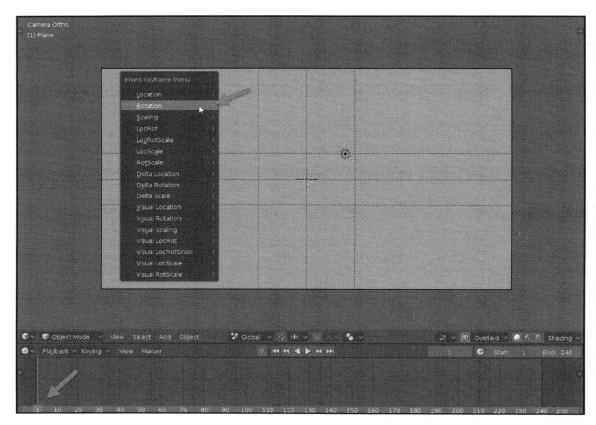

Move the playback head to 120 and add another rotation keyframe. Do not rotate your plane in the 3D View just yet.

Using the Graph Editor

In your timeline, change the editor setting to Graph Editor. This is a window where you can see all your animations as graphs. The horizontal lines represent the frames, with vertical values for properties. In this window, press the *N* key to open the sidebar containing all properties, as shown in the following screenshot:

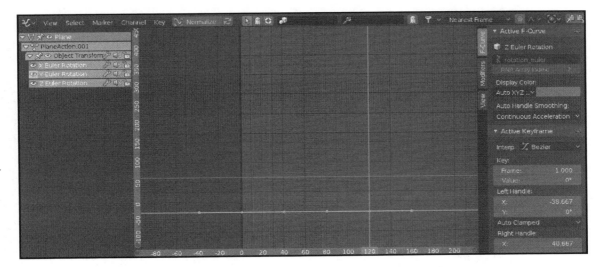

If you can't see all the information in the Graph Editor window, press the *Home* key on your keyboard to adjust your zoom. You can also use the **View** menu with the **View All** option.

On the left, in the sidebar, you can see all three transformation channels for the plane. Click on the small eye button for X and Y. That will disable viewing and changing that type of rotation, since we only want to deal with Z transformations. After that, left-click on **Z Euler Rotation** to see curves for that channel, as shown here:

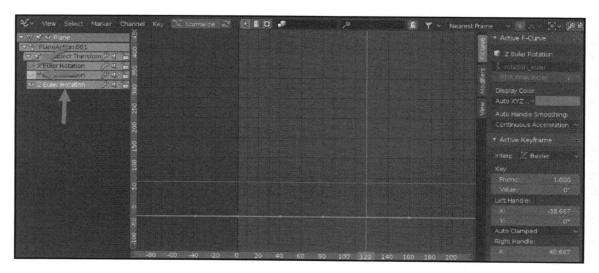

On the right-hand side, you will see the sidebar, which will display options for selected keyframes. Right-click on the small orange dot representing the first keyframe, and change the interpolation type in the F-Curve tab to **Linear**. You can also use the *V* key to set a keyframe to **Linear**, as shown here:

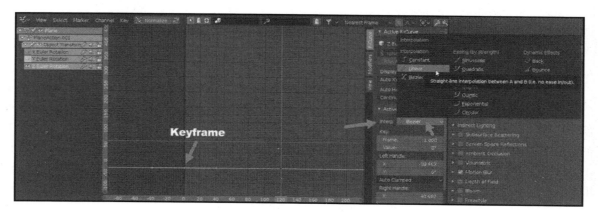

That will remove those dots on either side of your keyframe.

Select the second keyframe and repeat the same process, but making an additional edit. Once you change the type to **Linear**, you can set the **Value** for your keyframe to 360°, as follows:

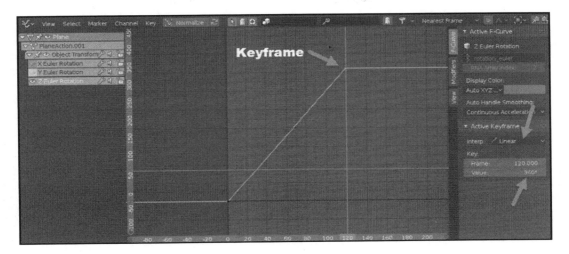

With those changes, you will see a straight line going up. If you press *Shift* + Spacebar to play your animation, you will see the plane spinning along the Z-axis.

But it will stop at frame 120. To make it go in a loop, you can add an animation modifier. In the properties tab, you can activate modifiers. We will add one called **Cycles**, as shown in the following screenshot:

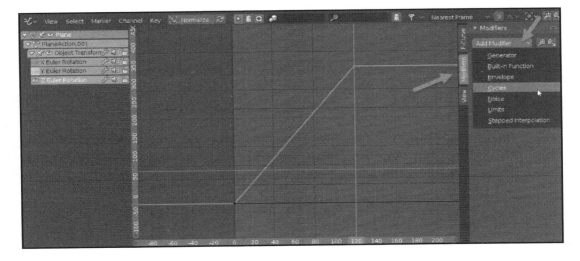

When you add **Cycles** to a curve, you will see that Blender loops all lines from your animation curves, as shown in the following screenshot. Press *Shift* + *Spacebar* again to see your endless rotation plane:

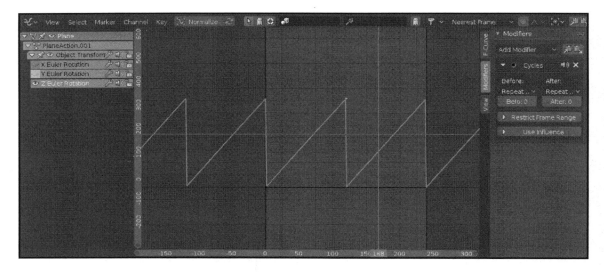

Using Eevee and the 3D View in Render mode will give you a great preview of how the video will look.

Rendering animations

We now have an animation ready to become a video file! Blender can render animations as video files, and even as image sequences. If you need the video file in a format such as MP4, you can create the video in such a format.

But, as a best practice for animation and video production, you should always create an image sequence first and later convert that to a video file, performing tests regarding compression and resolution.

You will find the settings to create your video as an MP4 file in the **Render** panel inside your properties window:

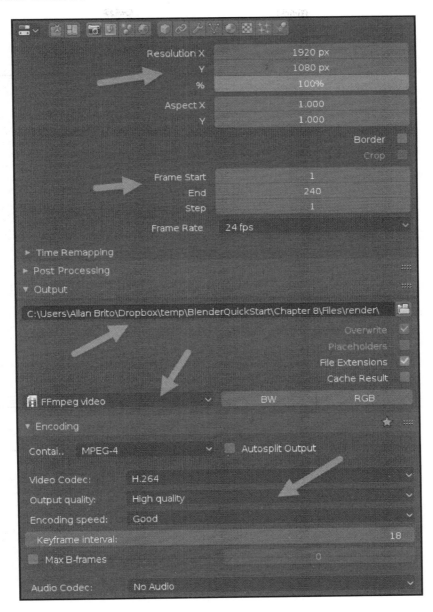

In the preceding screenshot, you can see at the top that we are using a resolution of 1920x 1080 pixels (FullHD). You can change that to 4096 × 2160 pixels for video in 4K.

In Eevee, in the post-processing options, you can turn on Motion Blur to get a better motion effect in your background.

The next setting in the preceding screenshot is about video length, which uses 1 as the starting frame and 240 as the last frame.

In the **Output** field, you have to choose a destination folder to which Blender will save your video file. Use the folder icon on the right to select the exact location. Also in the **Output** field, make sure you choose **FFmpeg video**.

Once you choose **FFmpeg**, the **Encoding** options will appear. There you can pick a container, which for an MP4 file must be MPEG-4, and the quality can be set to **High Quality**.

Using those settings will create an MP4 video file ready for YouTube.

To start the rendering process for a video, you have to press the *Ctrl + F12* keys, or use the **Render** menu and choose **Render Animation**, as shown here:

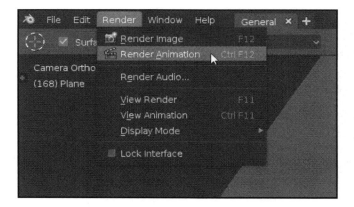

Depending on the settings and renderer, you may have to wait for a little while before Blender processes all frames. For long projects, it is perfectly reasonable for an animation of a few minutes to require several hours to process.

Rendering as an image sequence

What if you want to use an image sequence? The process to render an image sequence is the same as with an MP4 file, but you must choose PNG as the format from the file output settings, as follows:

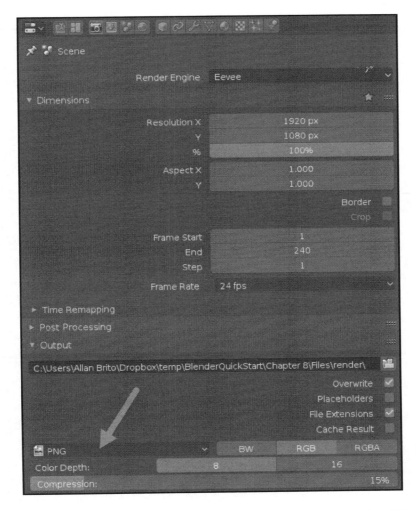

For MP4 files, you will eventually compress the data for your video and will have little room to reprocess the data. With a **PNG** file using lossless compression with no data loss, you can try to compress the project into MP4 in various formats.

Adding sound to animations

Where would an animation or video be without sound? In Blender, we can add audio to all types of project using a unique window called the video sequencer. In a nutshell, you will find that this window is a non-linear video editor inside Blender.

This is almost like having Adobe Premiere or Final Cut Pro inside Blender for video editing and cutting.

To show you how to add sound to animation, we can use the image sequence rendered in **PNG** from our intro animation.

The first thing to do after you have all the image files rendered is to open the video sequencer window. Use the space taken by the **Graph Editor**:

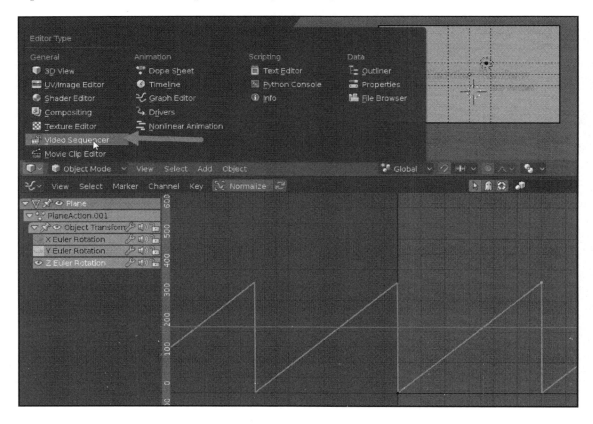

You will notice that this window is somewhat similar to the timeline with a few differences. On the left, you will see a channel list starting from zero and going up. These channels work like layers, where you can compose multiple tracks of video on top of each other, as seen in the following screenshot.

Below the horizontal line, you will see the animation time, and at the top, you can see a preview of your video by using the **Backdrop** option:

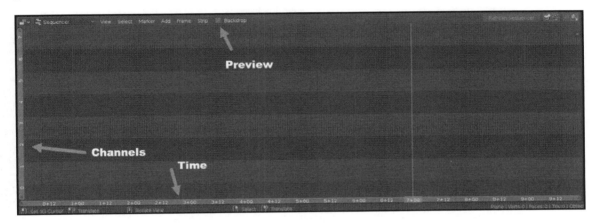

To add our image sequence to the editor, you must use the **Add** menu and choose **Image**, as shown in the following screenshot. Inside the file selector option, you can press the *A* key to select all files from the folder where you rendered the images:

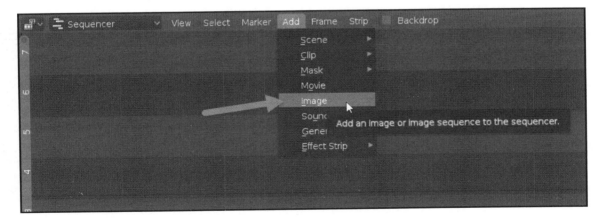

Once you add the image sequence, Blender will create something called a strip. That is what it calls the video block containing all images from the sequence. You can use the *G* key to move it around. Blender will display the frame number where you place the strip to guide you around.

Notice that at the beginning and end of a strip you will have two arrows. If you select those arrows, you can also resize the strip:

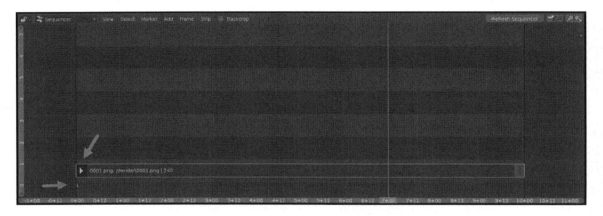

 Like all other parts of Blender, you can use the same shortcuts to select and manipulate elements in the video sequencer.

Make sure you place your strip starting on frame 1 and ending at 240. Now, to add a sound or music, you can use the same **Add** menu and choose **Sound**. Locate an MP3 file you like and import it to the project.

You can download public domain music from the resources for this chapter to use in your project.

Move the sound strip until it is at the same alignment as your image sequence. With the audio strip still selected, move the playback head to 240, and in the **Strip** menu choose **Cut (Hard) at frame**, as shown here:

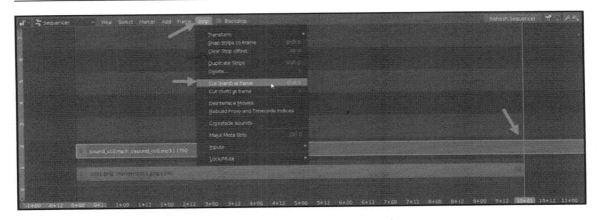

If you take a closer look at the music used for this project, you will see that each strip displays the total number of frames right next to the filename. The animation has 240 frames, and our music has 1,792. We have to cut the music to remove all unnecessary content from position 240 until the end.

This is the same procedure used to cut video, if you want to use Blender to edit external video as well.

After cutting the music, you can select the end part of your strip and delete it from your editor as follows:

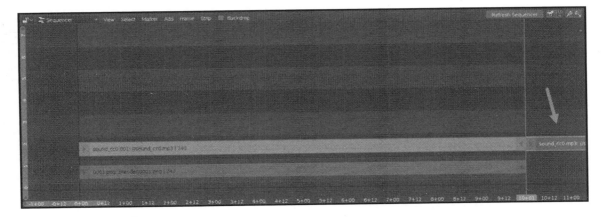

Rendering a finished video

At this point, if you hit *Shift* + Spacebar to play your animation, you will see a preview of all motion with the music in the background. The next step is to render the results as an MP4 file.

You can use the same settings that we used previously in this chapter to create an MP4 file. The difference now is that you must choose an audio codec for your file. An excellent choice for an MP4 file is **AAC**, as shown here:

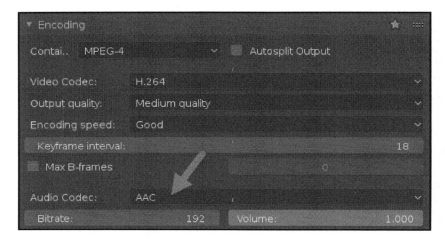

Whenever you have strips or content in the video sequencer, Blender will process that information as render output. You don't have to do anything different—simply having something in the video sequencer will make Blender ignore anything in the 3D View.

To disable this and make Blender render the 3D View, you can turn off the **Sequencer** option in the **Render** panel, as shown here:

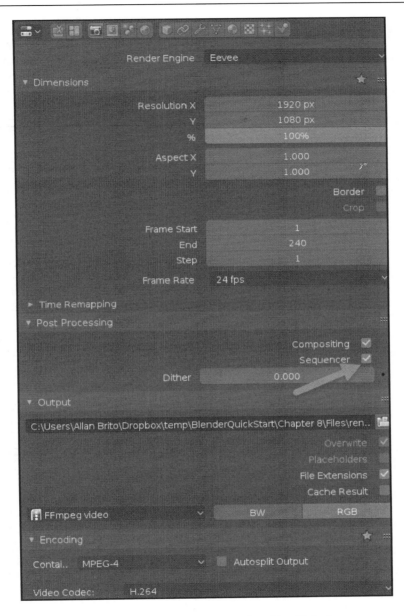

Now you are ready to upload your video with sound to YouTube!

Summary

You now have a great set of tools in Blender to create animations and videos using loops and including an audio soundtrack.

The next step from here is to look for better ways to put your creativity to work and make some animation and video projects with the software, such as making some intro videos for commercial or personal videos.

That is a great start, but only scratches the surface of what Blender can do for animations and video.

Other Books You May Enjoy

If you enjoyed this book, you may be interested in these other books by Packt:

Unity Virtual Reality Projects - Second Edition
Jonathan Linowes

ISBN: 9781788478809

- Create 3D scenes with Unity and other 3D tools while learning about world space and scale
- Build and run VR applications for specific headsets, including Oculus, Vive, and Daydream
- Interact with virtual objects using eye gaze, hand controllers, and user input events
- Move around your VR scenes using locomotion and teleportation
- Implement an audio fireball game using physics and particle systems
- Implement an art gallery tour with teleportation and data info
- Design and build a VR storytelling animation with a soundtrack and timelines
- Create social VR experiences with Unity networking

Building an RPG with Unity 2018 - Second Edition

Vahé Karamian

ISBN: 9781788623469

- Construct a framework for inventory, equipment, characters, enemies, quests, and game events
- Understand how to load and unload scenes and assets
- Create multiplayer game settings for your RPG
- Design a UI for user input and feedback
- Implement AI for non-character players
- Customize your character at runtime

Leave a review - let other readers know what you think

Please share your thoughts on this book with others by leaving a review on the site that you bought it from. If you purchased the book from Amazon, please leave us an honest review on this book's Amazon page. This is vital so that other potential readers can see and use your unbiased opinion to make purchasing decisions, we can understand what our customers think about our products, and our authors can see your feedback on the title that they have worked with Packt to create. It will only take a few minutes of your time, but is valuable to other potential customers, our authors, and Packt. Thank you!

Index

Made in the USA
Lexington, KY
25 November 2018